joe bonamassa
blues deluxe

This book was approved by Joe Bonamassa

Transcribed by Paul Pappas, Steve Gorenberg, and Andrew Moore

Cherry Lane Music Company
Director of Publications/Project Editor: Mark Phillips
Project Coordinator: Rebecca Skidmore

ISBN 978-1-60378-102-2

Visit our website at www.cherrylaneprint.com

joe bonamassa
blues deluxe

Joe Bonamassa was born May 8, 1977. If that seems like a trivial way to introduce his first full-blooded blues album, consider that, by many historical estimates, that day would have been Robert Johnson's 66th birthday. That's more than a coincidence, as one listen to *Blues Deluxe* demonstrates. Though only in his mid-20s, Joe's fluid, passionate, jaw-dropping guitar belies an innate sense of the blues greater than his years. Indeed, before Joe could vote, drive a car, or even attend junior high, he was a blues guitarist of such talent and potential that he caught the attention of B.B. King. As a teenager, he shared stages with King, Albert Collins, John Lee Hooker, and other patriarchs of the electric guitar. It's beyond question there's an old bluesman's soul in Joe Bonamassa.

Joe's previous two albums, the critically praised, classic-rock-influenced *A New Day Yesterday* and *So, It's Like That* (a #1 *Billboard* blues album), focused on his burgeoning ability to craft and sing concise rock anthems. Nevertheless, Joe's blues spirit shone through each. At his incendiary live performances, fans hung on every note of his acrobatic, blood-pumping solos, often expressing their desire to see Joe delve even deeper into his Delta roots.

Returning home from nearly two years of non-stop touring, Bonamassa hit the studio to "blow off some steam" and flex his blues muscles… just to see where it led. The results of the sessions that followed floored everyone who heard them. Paying tribute to mentors like King, Collins, and Hooker, as well as blues legends like Buddy Guy, Elmore James, T-Bone Walker, Freddie King, Robert Johnson, and British Invasion blues/rock deity Jeff Beck, Bonamassa takes the styles of his predecessors and shows just how much he's learned—and just how much further he can take it.

Blues Deluxe marks Joe's emergence as one of the greatest roots musicians on the road today. The blues has a long and vibrant history with a mythology and a cast of characters all its own. With this album, Joe Bonamassa proves himself the latest legend-in-waiting on that continuum.

His soulful vocals complement the sweat-soaked passion of his guitar, an instrument he plays with equal eloquence on quick-finger shuffles and tension building wailers. Echoes of B.B. King, Albert King, Stevie Ray Vaughan, and others are there, but Joe's forward-looking style takes unexpected turns into new scales, new riffs, new mind-blowing, finger-cramping pyrotechnics. And while his musicianship is impeccable, he never loses touch with the raw emotion that makes the blues what it is.

The United States Congress declared 2003 as the Year of the Blues, celebrating the 100th anniversary of W. C. Handy's inspiration to bring this vital music to mainstream America. This album is Joe Bonamassa's stellar contribution to the celebration, a party he's been throwing for himself and his fans since he was 12 years old.

Look out, because the Year of the Blues is getting the *Deluxe* treatment.
—Harris Cohen, 2003

It's now 2009 and Joe Bonamassa has released nine albums, the latest being *The Ballad of John Henry*. After the release of the *Best of Joe Bonamassa* songbook, we heard from Joe's fans. You wanted matching books. We started with *Blues Deluxe* because it's been a consistent fan favorite over the years. We also heard from you because of a misprint that left many expecting "Pain and Sorrow" to appear in the first book. We rectify that situation here and include it as a bonus in *Blues Deluxe*.
Enjoy.
—John Stix, 2009

CONTENTS

YOU UPSET ME BABY

Words and Music by
B.B. King and Jules Bihari

Intro
Medium Shuffle ♩ = 126

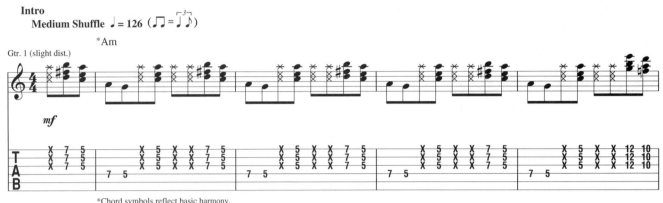

*Chord symbols reflect basic harmony.

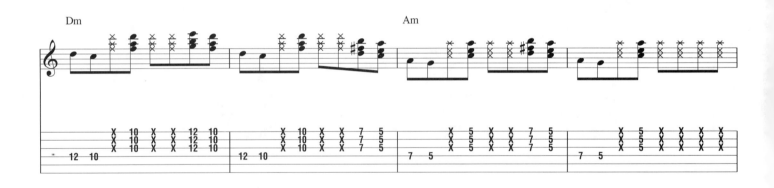

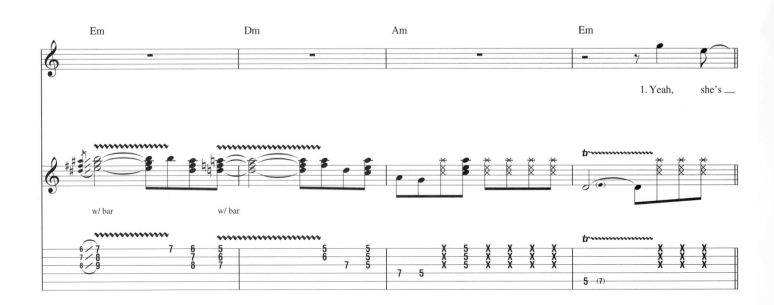

1. Yeah, she's

Verse

3rd time, Gtr. 1: w/ Rhy. Fill 1

_____ thir - ty - six in the bust, _____ for - ty - eight in the _____ waist, for - ty - four hips. She's got real _____
_____ not _____ too tall, com - plex - ion is fair. Man, she knocks me out the way she _____
_____ hard to de - scribe _____ her, it's hard to start. _____ Nev - er stop, no, _____ be - cause I've _____

_____ cra - zy legs. _____
_____ wear _____ her hair. _____ You up - set me, ba - by. Yes, _____
_____ got a weak heart.

_____ you up - set me, ba - by. Like _____ get - ting hit by a fall - ing tree,

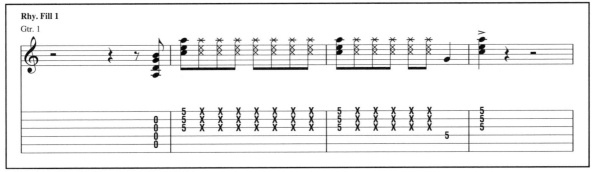

Rhy. Fill 1

Gtr. 1

5

3. Yeah, it's ___

D.S. al Coda

8

Yeah, _____ ba - by, _____ right now. _____

BURNING HELL

Words and Music by
John Lee Hooker
and Bernard Besman

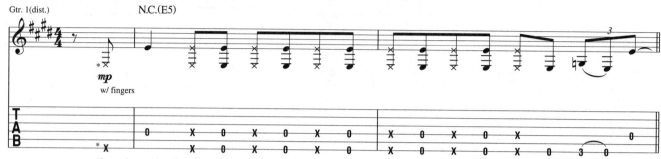

Open E tuning:
(low to high) E-B-E-G♯-B-E

Intro
Moderately fast Shuffle ♩ = 168

Gtr. 1(dist.)

N.C.(E5)

*Percussive sound produced by tapping strings with tips of right-hand fingers.

1. Hey, ____

Verse
N.C.(E5)

____ ev - 'ry-bod-y talk a - bout it, burn-ing hell, ____ burn-ing hell. ____

Copyright © 1970 by Universal Music - Careers and Sony/ATV Music Publishing LLC
Copyright Renewed
All Rights on behalf of Sony/ATV Music Publishing LLC Administered by Sony/ATV Music Publishing LLC, 8 Music Square West, Nashville, TN 37203
International Copyright Secured All Rights Reserved

10

Ain't no hell ____ but a burn-ing hell. ____

Interlude

N.C.(E5)

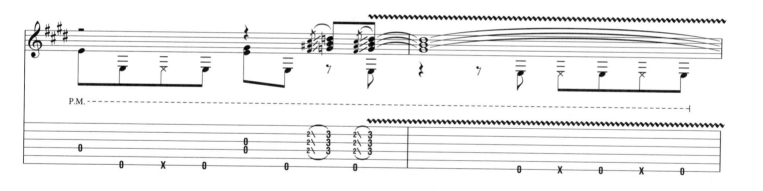

2. When I die, __

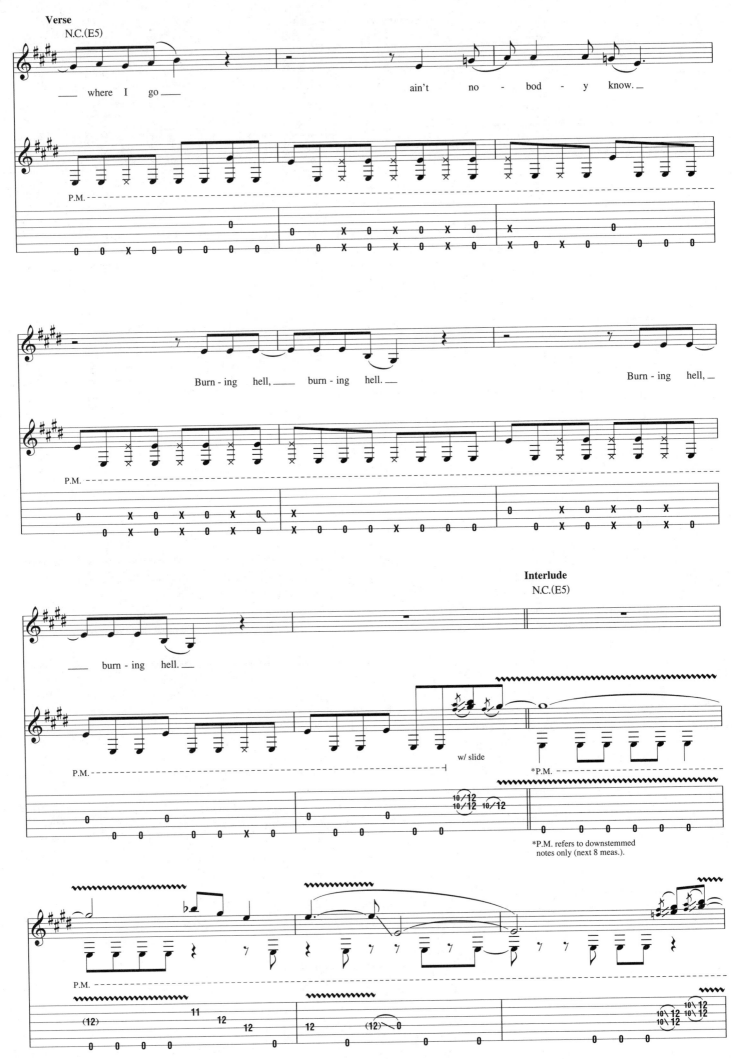

Interlude
N.C.(E5)

prayed for me.

w/ slide

P.M. - - - - - - - - - - - - - -

*P.M. - - - - - - - - - - - - -

*As before (next 7 meas.)

Well. _____

P.M. - - - - - - - - - - -

P.M. -

Verse
N.C.(E5)

4. I went down _____ to the church _ house.

I got down _

w/o slide

P.M. - - - - - - - - - - - -

14

on my bend-ed knee, ___ and I begged ___ Dea-con Jones, ___

"Won't you pray ___ for me?" ___ He said, "Son, ___

___ take my hand." ___ He said, "Son, ___ take my hand. ___

Yeah, you're hav - ing a burn-ing hell. You're hav -

grad. cresc.

-ing   a   burn-ing   hell.   You're hav -   ing   a   burn-ing   hell.

Interlude
N.C.

Burn-ing   hell!"

w/ pick   w/ slide   f

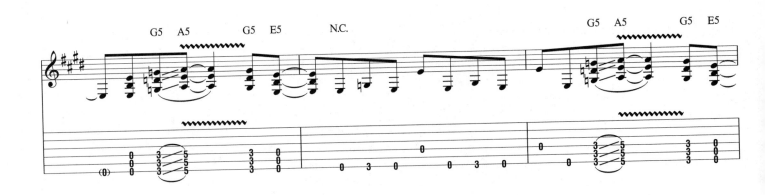

G5   A5   G5   E5   N.C.   G5   A5   G5   E5

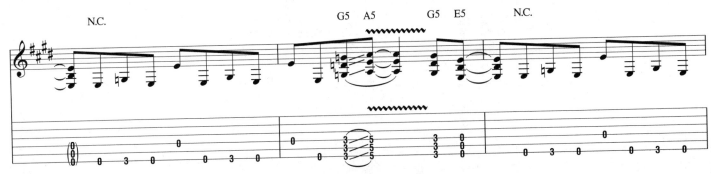

N.C.   G5   A5   G5   E5   N.C.

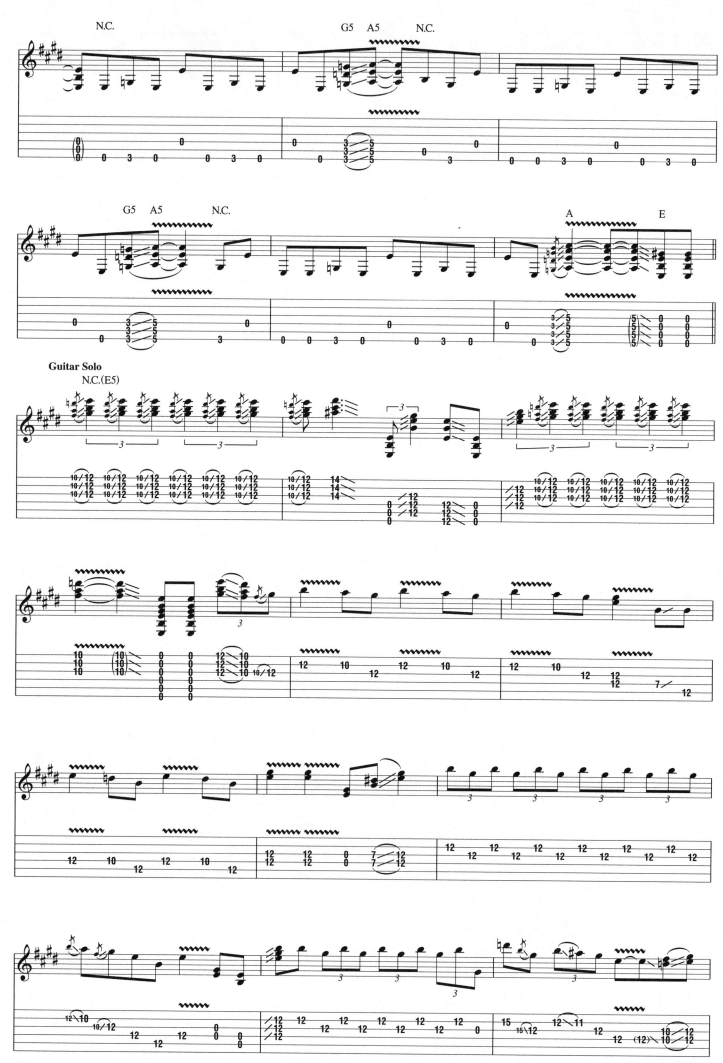

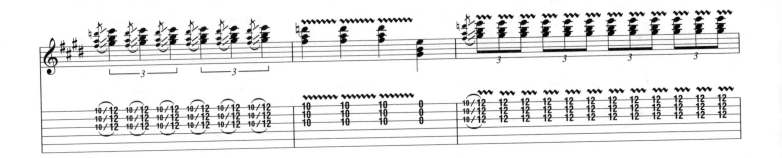

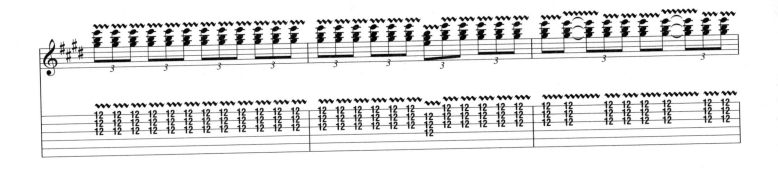

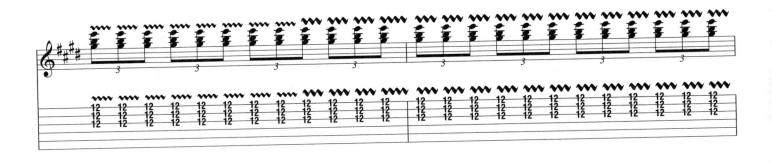

*steady gliss.

*Slide up strings in steady gliss. while strumming eighth-note triplet rhythm.

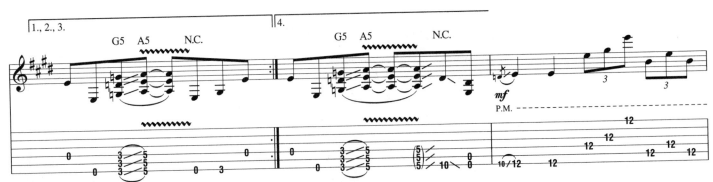

Burn - ing hell, _____ burn - ing hell. _____

Burn - ing hell, _____

grad. cresc.

_____ burn - ing hell. _____

Burn - ing hell! _____

w/ pick

Interlude

E5   N.C.   G5   A5   G5   E5

w/ slide   *f*

G5   E5   G5   E5   G5   A5   G5   E5   N.C.   G5   E5

Don't _ know   why. _____   Don't _ know   why.

25

Oh. _____

Outro-Harmonica Solo

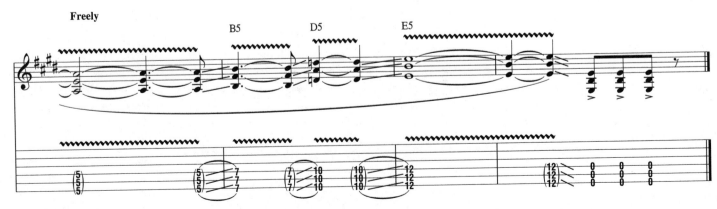

BLUES DELUXE

Words and Music by
Jeffrey Rod

Intro
Slow Blues ♩. = 50

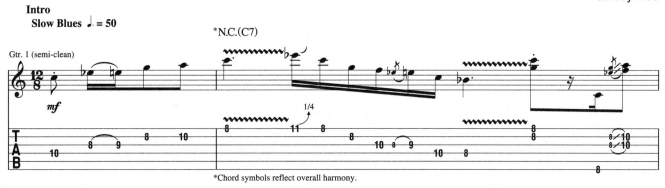

*Chord symbols reflect overall harmony.

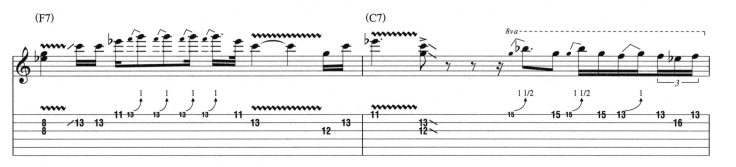

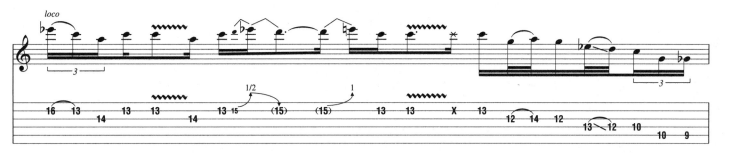

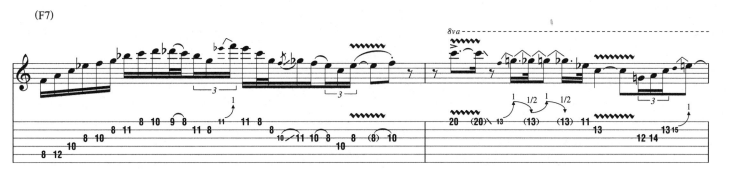

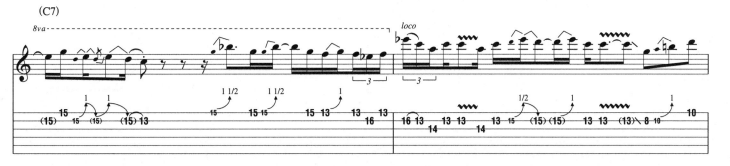

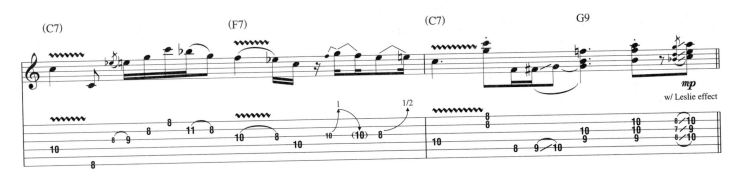

Verse

1. I don't know__ too__ much a - bout__ love,__ ba - by _____ now, ____ but I sure__

think I've got _____ it bad, ____ yeah. ____

I don't know __ too __ much a-bout __ love, __ ba - by _____ now, __ but I sure __

think I've got _____ it bad. ____ yeah. _____

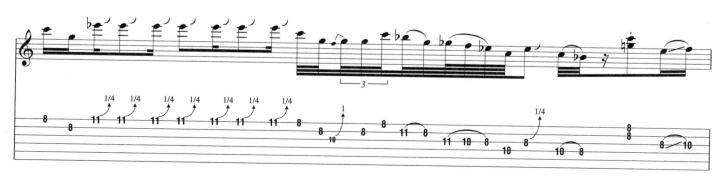

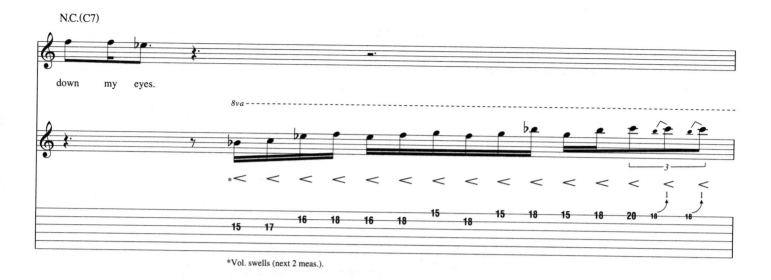

down   my   eyes.

*Vol. swells (next 2 meas.).

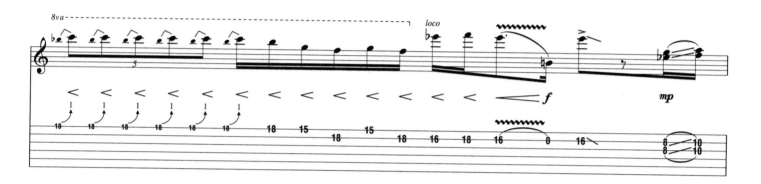

As   I   sit here in my lone - ly room, ___ now, ___   tears _____ go - in'

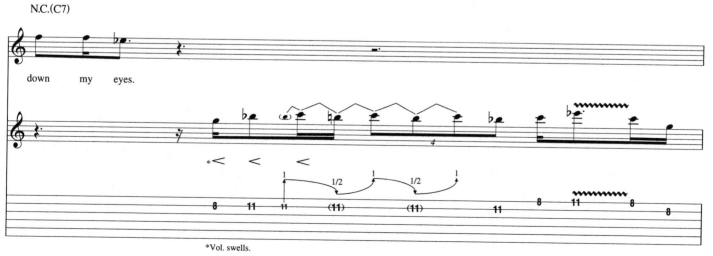

down   my   eyes.

*Vol. swells.

G7

I won-der how you could treat me so low down and dirt-y.

F9

You know what? Your heart must be made

N.C.(C7)   (F7)

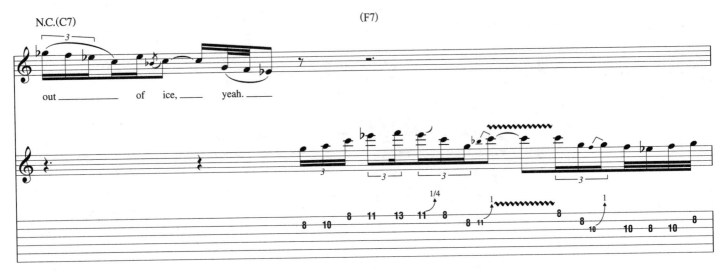

out _____ of ice, _____ yeah. _____

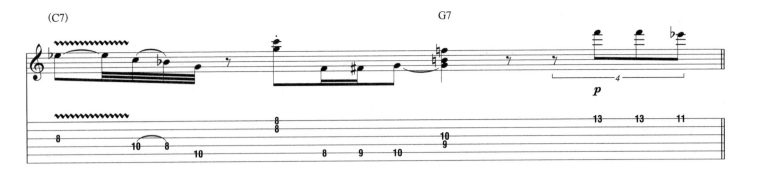

Guitar Solo

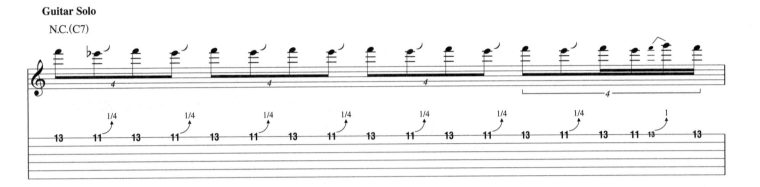

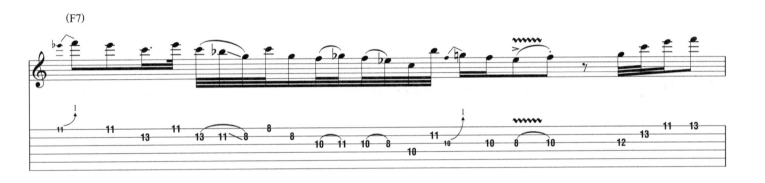

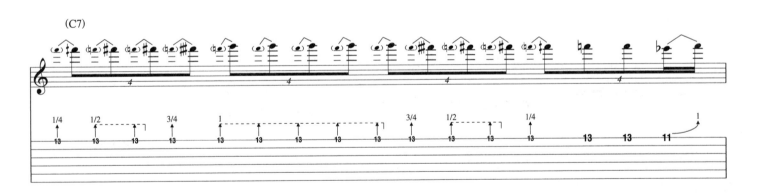

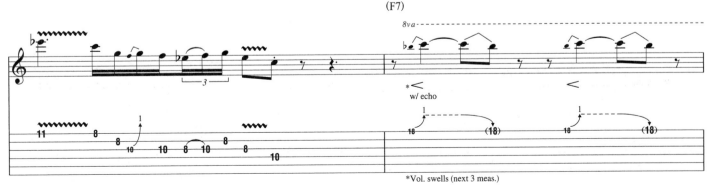

*Vol. swells (next 3 meas.)

35

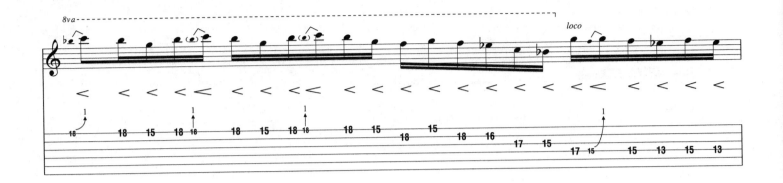

(C7)

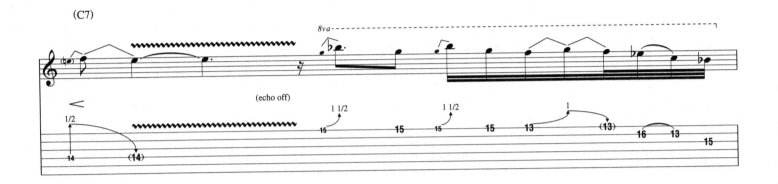

loco

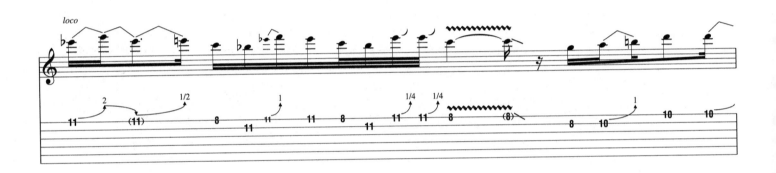

(G7)

(F7)

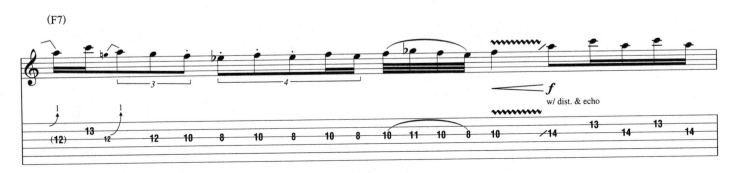

36

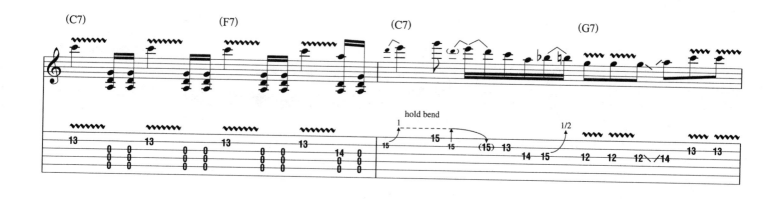

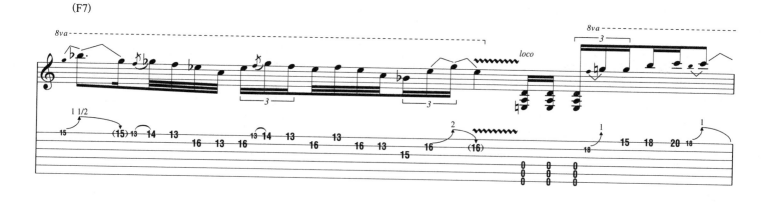

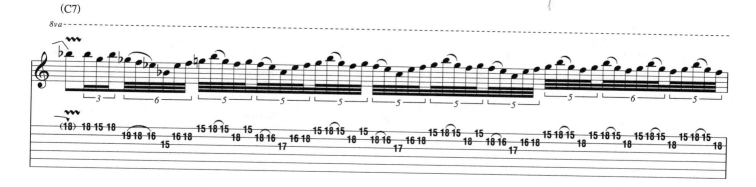

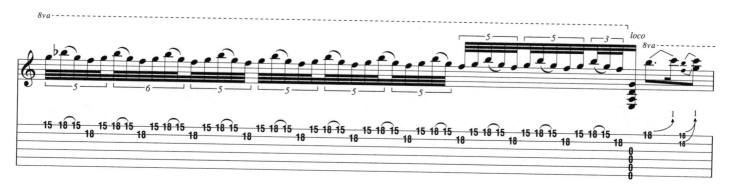

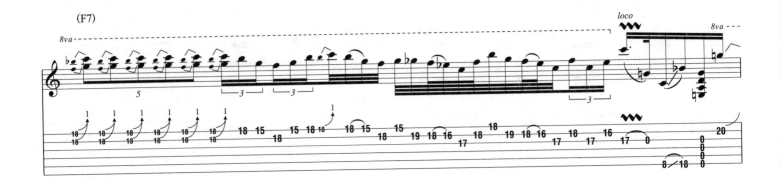

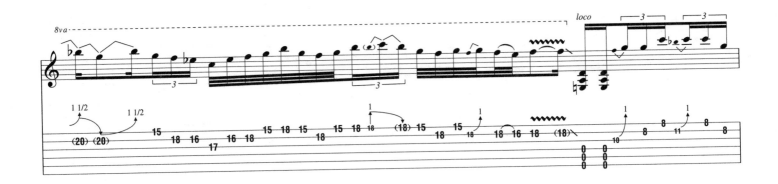

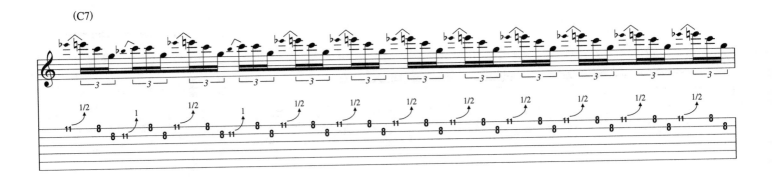

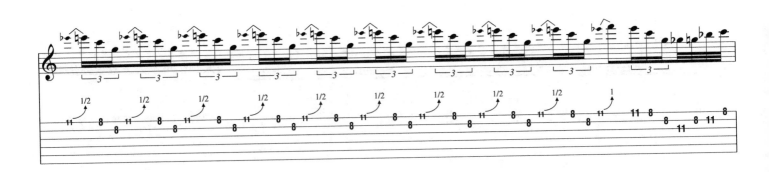

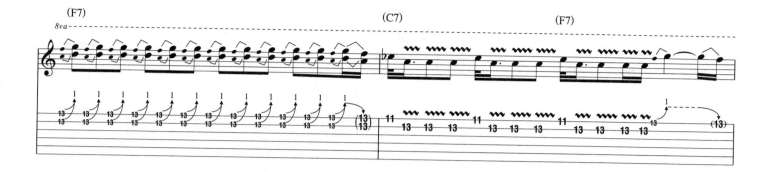

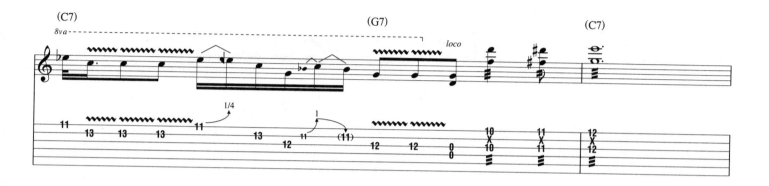

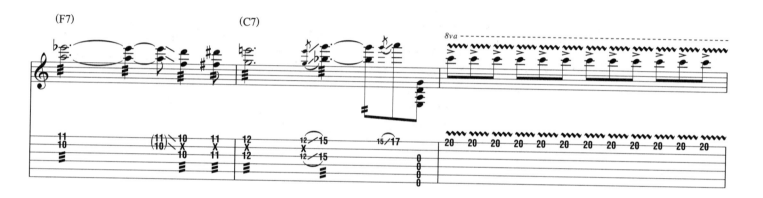

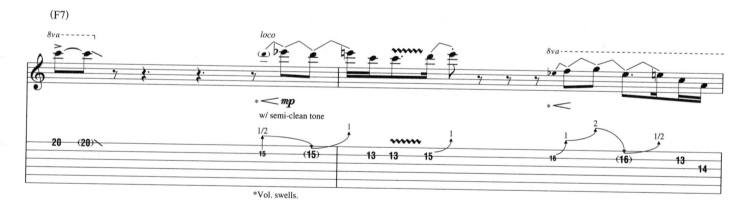

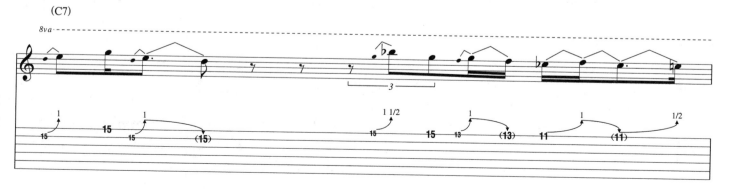

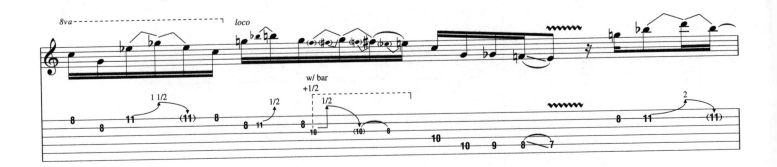

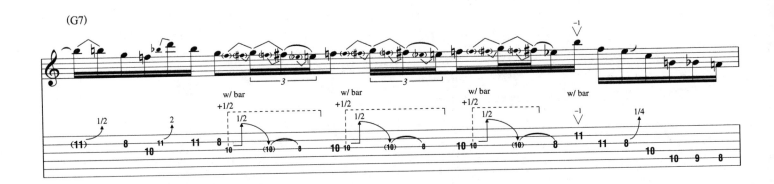

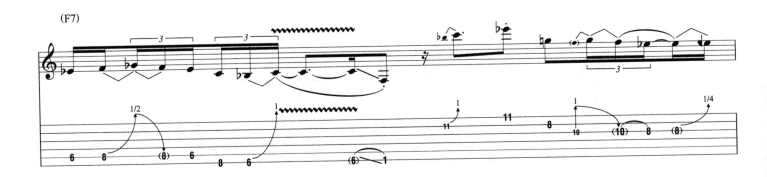

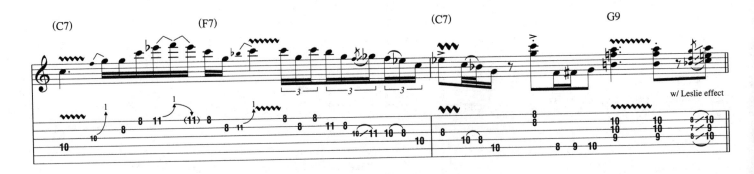

Verse

3. Some - times I ___ get so ___ wor - ried, ba - by ___ now, ___ you know, I wan - na

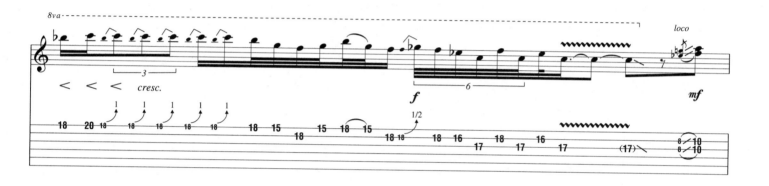

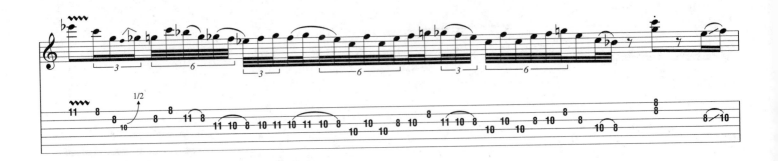

Free time

'Cause I don't know too much a-bout love,_____ babe,_____ but I sure_____ think I,_____

Tempo I

sure_____ think I got_____ it bad,_____ yeah._____

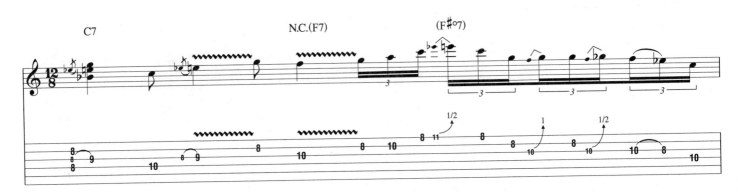

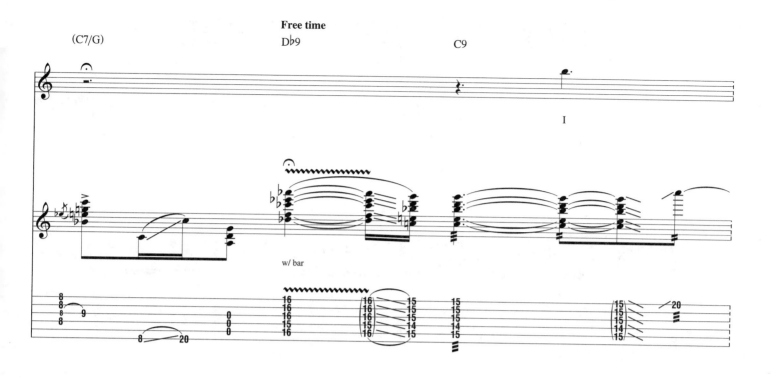

sure think I've got it bad, _____ yeah. _____

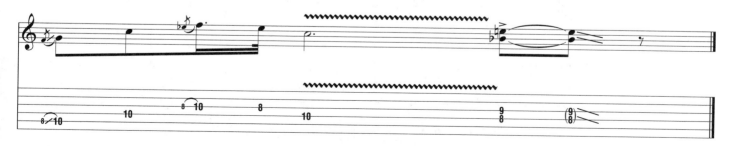

MAN OF MANY WORDS

Written by
Buddy Guy

*Chord symbols reflect overall harmony.

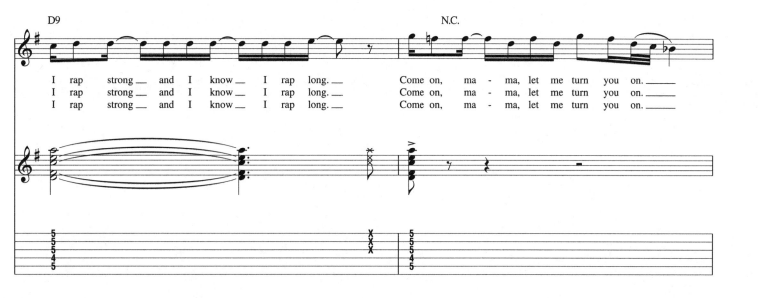

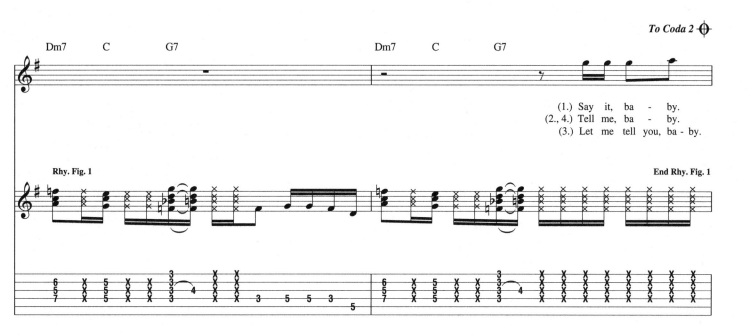

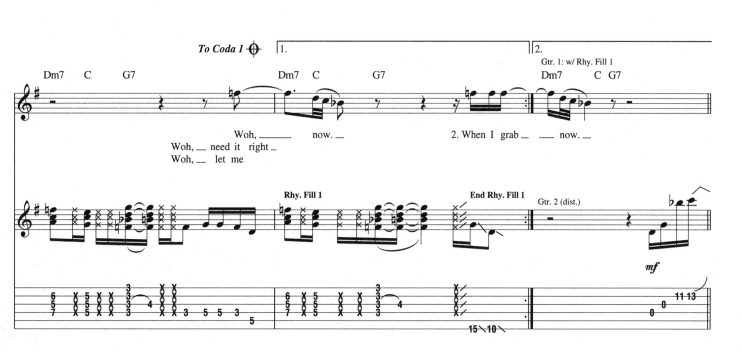

Guitar Solo

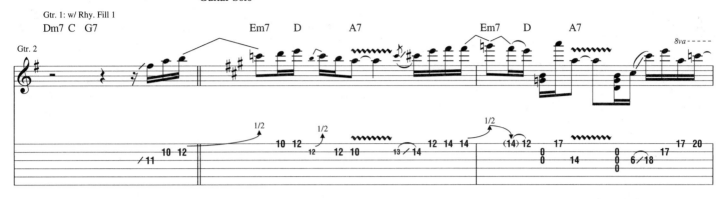

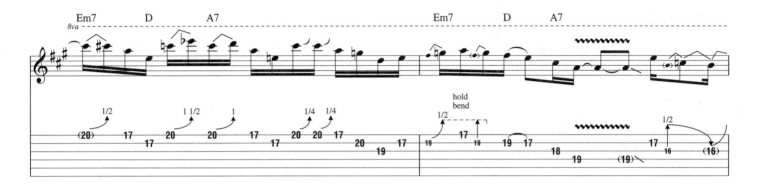

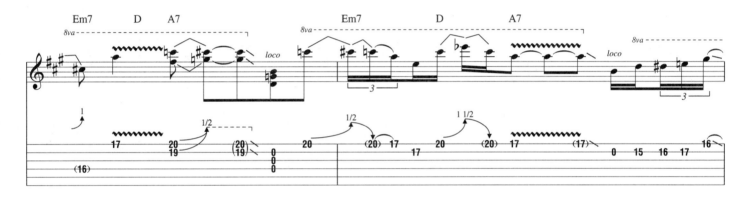

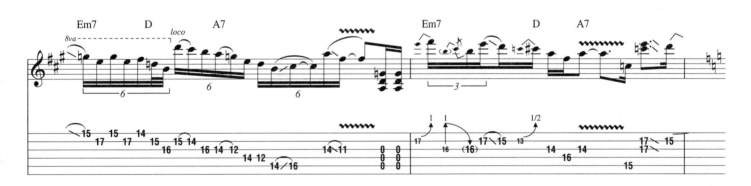

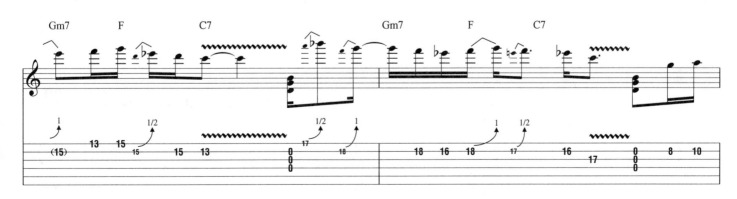

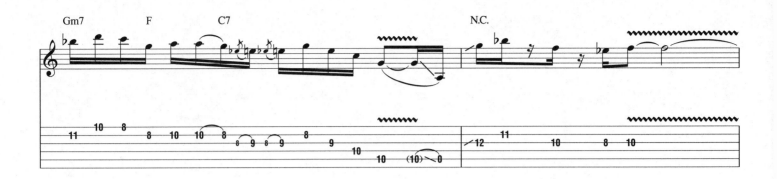

Interlude
Gtr. 2 tacet
N.C.(G7)

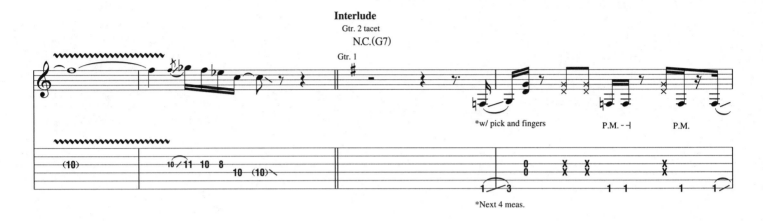

Gtr. 1

*w/ pick and fingers P.M. ┘ P.M.

*Next 4 meas.

D.S. al Coda 2

P.M. ----┘ P.M. P.M. P.M.

 Coda 2

Gtr. 1: w/ Rhy. Fig. 1

Oh, ____ let me turn you on _____ now, __ ba - by.

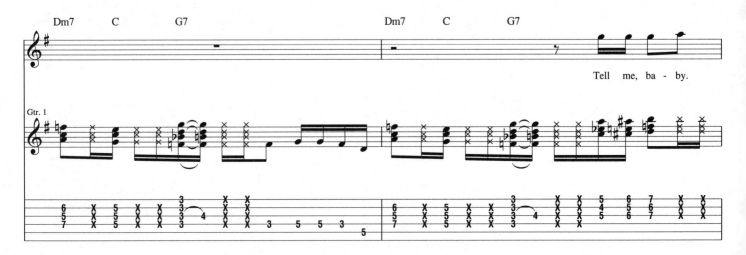

Tell me, ba - by.

Gtr. 1

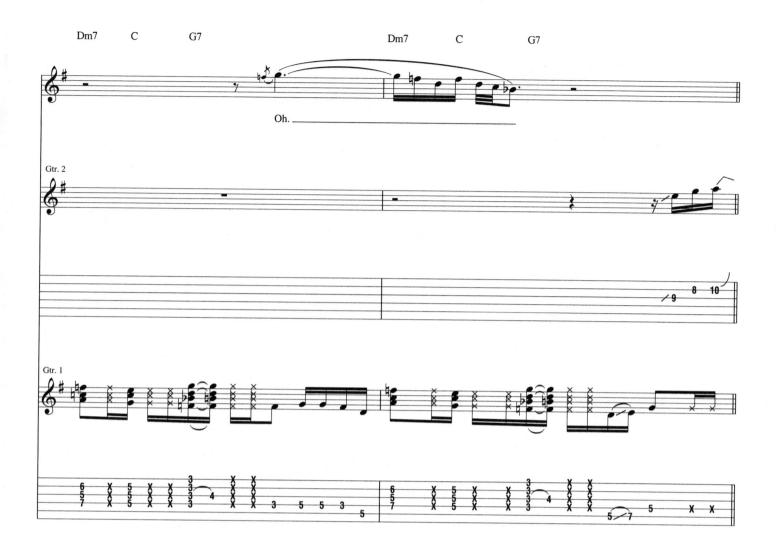

Oh. _____

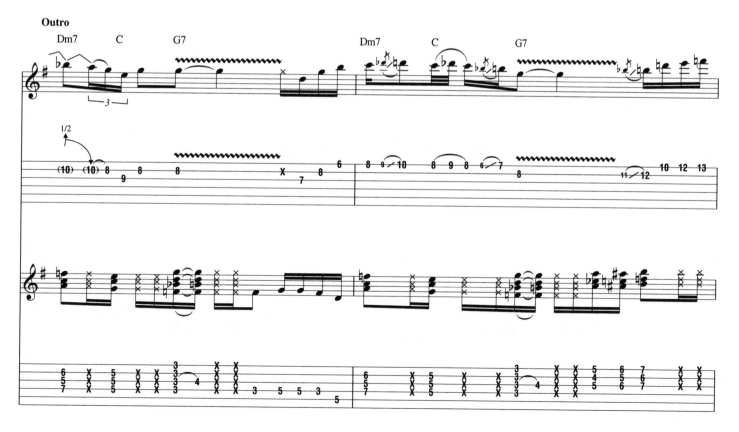

Outro

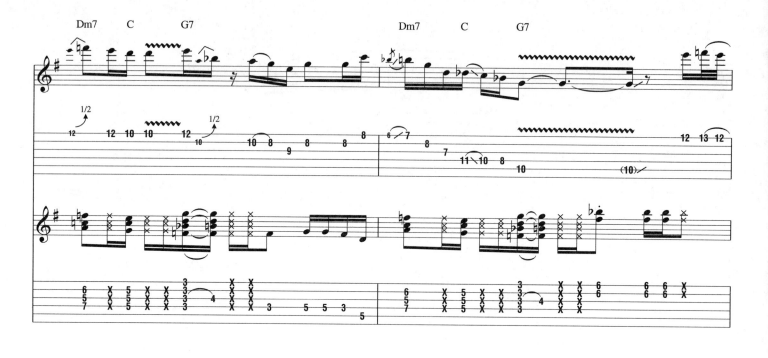

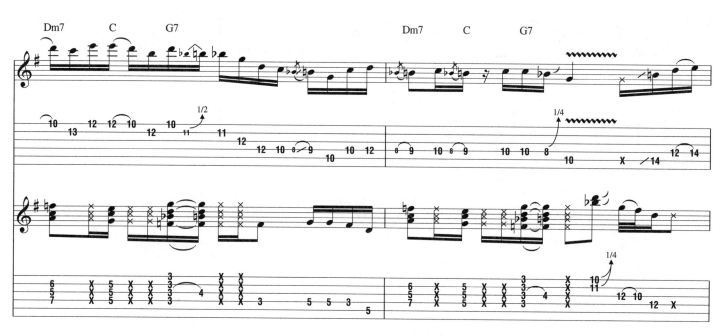

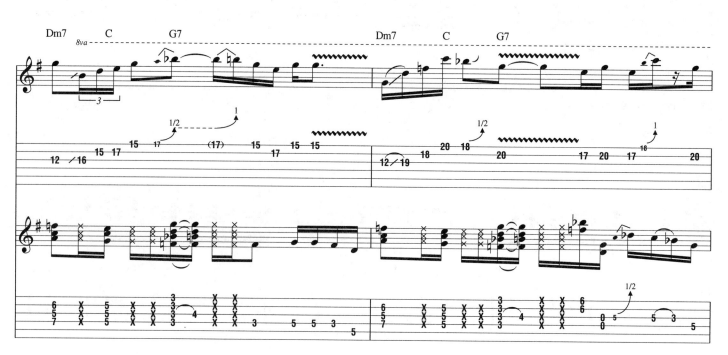

WOKE UP DREAMING

Words and Music by
Joe Bonamassa and Will Jennings

Tune down 1 step:
(low to high) D-G-C-F-A-D

Intro
Fast ♩ = 160

1. Woke	up dream - in' I was gon - na die.
2. Reached	out for ___ her and she was not there.
3. Dev - il's	ris - in'; you don't have a chance.
4. I	just want ___ to live an - oth - er day.

Woke up dream - in' I was gon - na die.

All my

sins a - bound me; it's my turn to cry.

Yeah.

Interlude

54

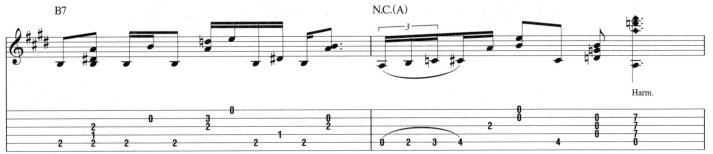

2nd time, D.S. al Coda
(take repeat)

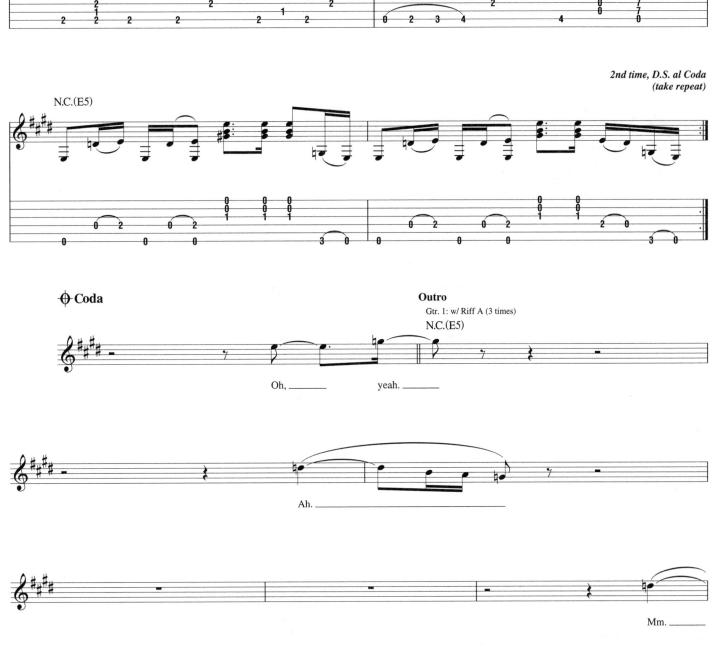

I DON'T LIVE ANYWHERE

Words and Music by
Joe Bonamassa and
Michael Himelstein

*Chord symbols reflect overall harmony.

Verse

This road is my home.

WILD ABOUT YOU BABY

Words and Music by
Elmore James

Open D tuning:
(low to high) D-A-D-F#-A-D

Intro
Moderate Shuffle ♩ = 120

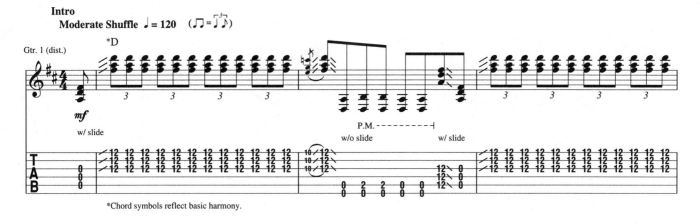

*Chord symbols reflect basic harmony.

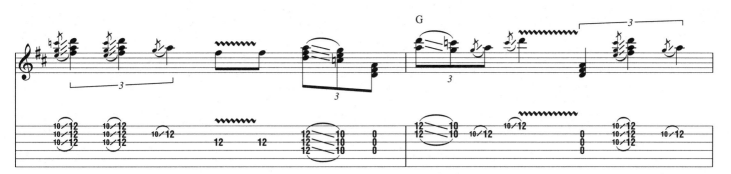

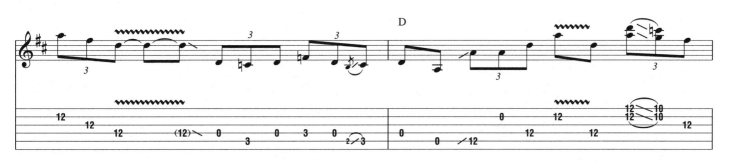

and I hope___ you come back home.___

Yeah,___

Guitar Solo

yeah.

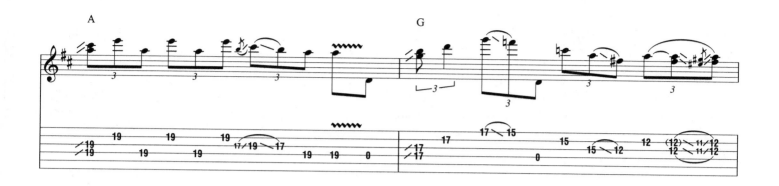

Verse

leave me, ba - by, ___ and you know you done me ___ wrong. ___

Yes, you ___ leave me, ba - by, and I know you done me ___

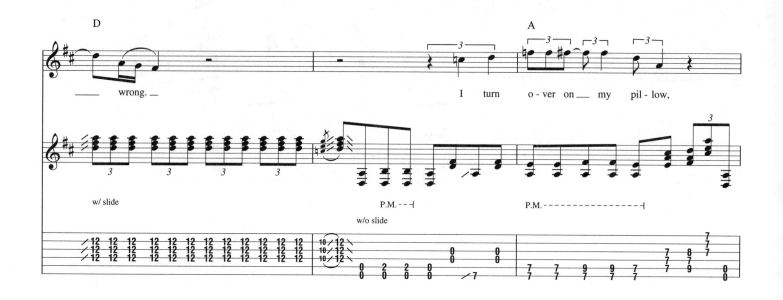

wrong.

I turn o-ver on ___ my pil-low,

w/ slide

w/o slide

P.M.

P.M.

and I hope ___ you come back ___ home. ___

Oh, ___ look out, babe.

w/ slide

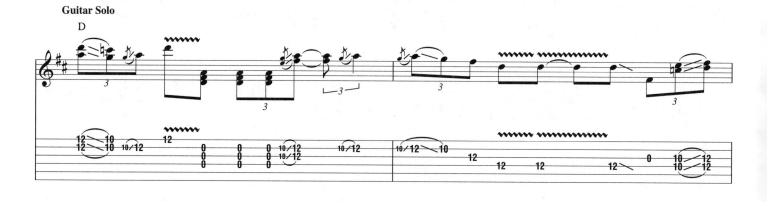

Guitar Solo

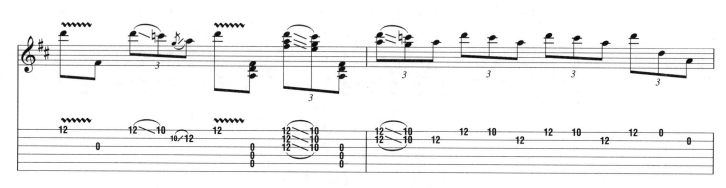

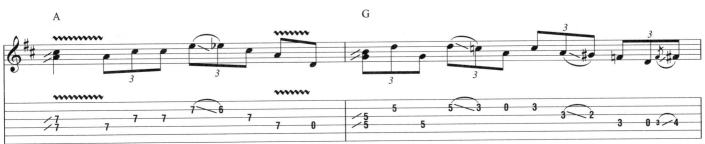

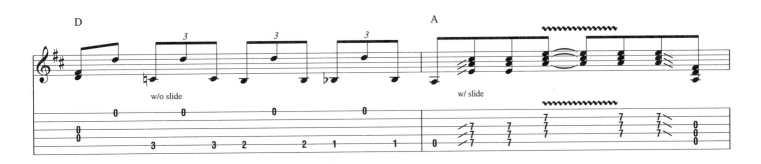

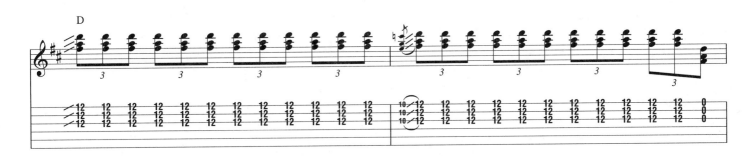

good - bye now, ba - by,   I hope I nev - er see you an - y - more. ____

70

LONG DISTANCE BLUES

Words and Music by
Bernice Carter

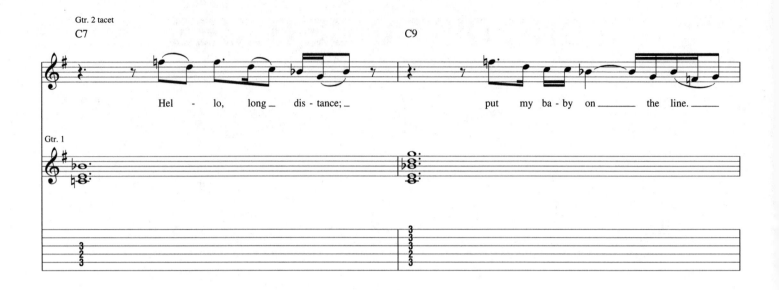

Hel - lo, long _ dis - tance; _ put my ba - by on _____ the line. _____

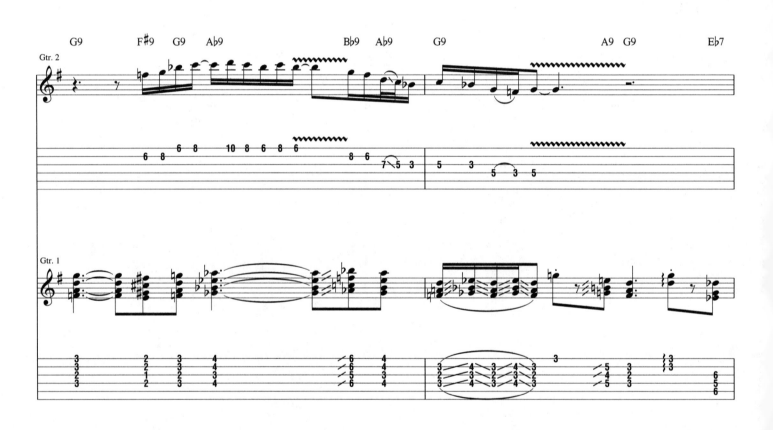

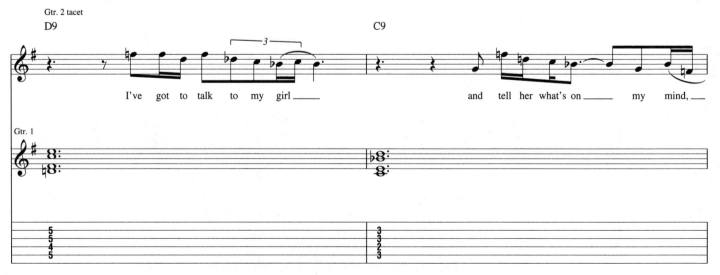

I've got to talk to my girl _____ and tell her what's on _____ my mind, _____

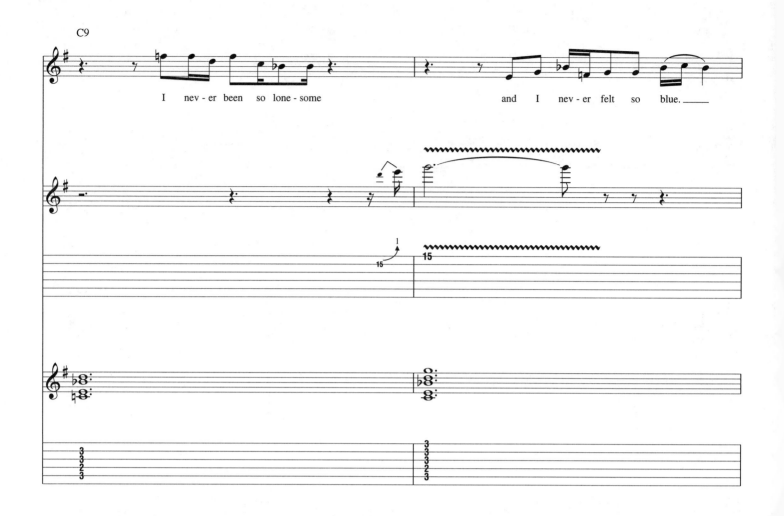

C9

I nev-er been so lone-some   and I nev-er felt so blue. _____

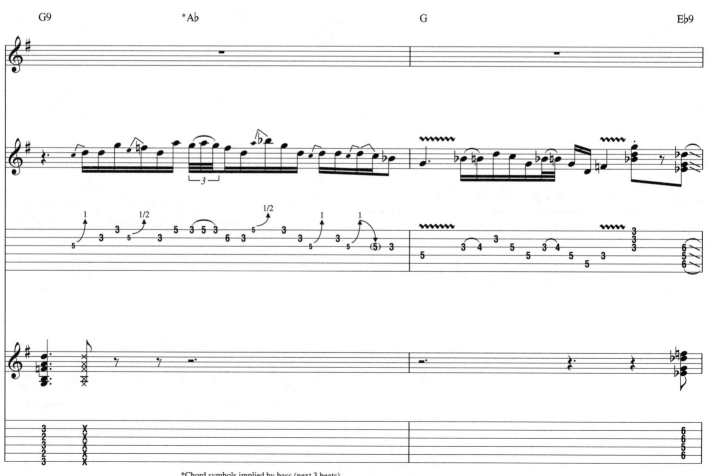

G9   *A♭   G   E♭9

*Chord symbols implied by bass (next 3 beats).

Well, it's been a long time, ba - by, __ since I got a let - ter from you. __

w/ dist.

Guitar Solo

Gtr. 1 tacet

Gtr. 2

*Chord symbols implied by bass (next 12 meas.).

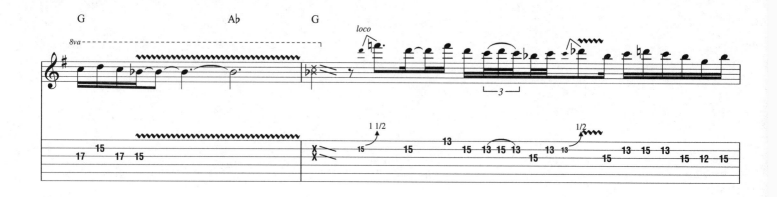

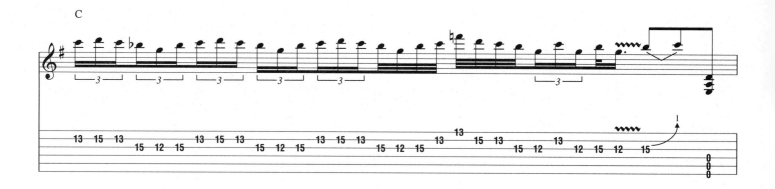

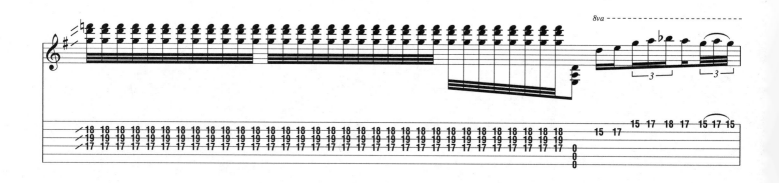

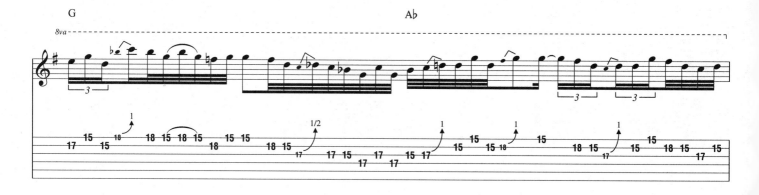

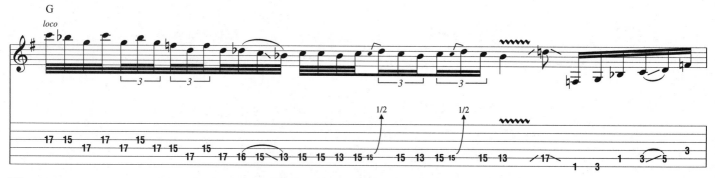

PACK IT UP

Words and Music by
Geoffrey Beadle, Ronald Carthy,
George Chandler, Wilfred Davies,
Michael Eve, Gabriel Gregory,
Delisle Harper, Goldin Hunte
and Christopher Mercer

Gtr. 2: w/ Riff A

2.

Interlude

N.C.

Guitar Solo

Db9   Eb9

Gtr. 2

Gtr. 1

Rhy. Fig. 1

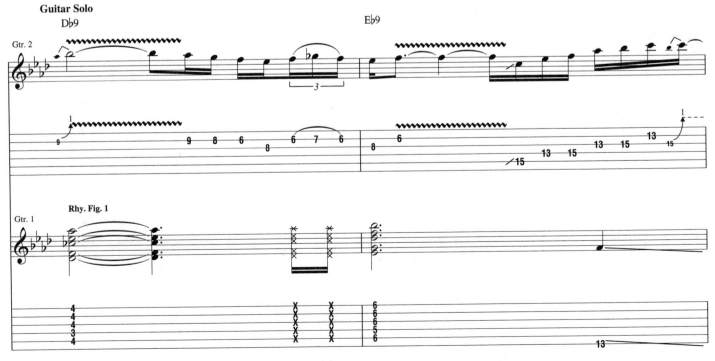

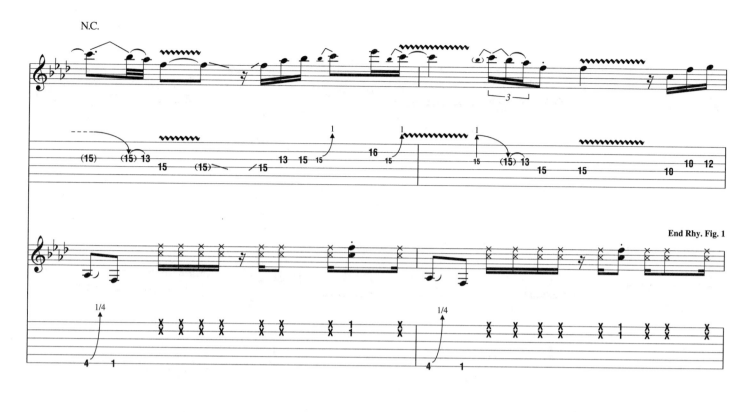

Gtr. 1: w/ Rhy. Fig. 1 (1 1/2 times)

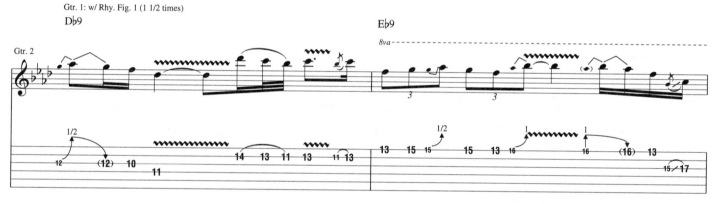

N.C.

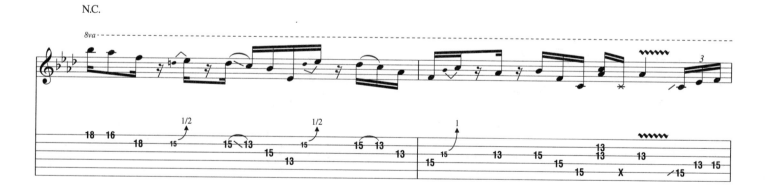

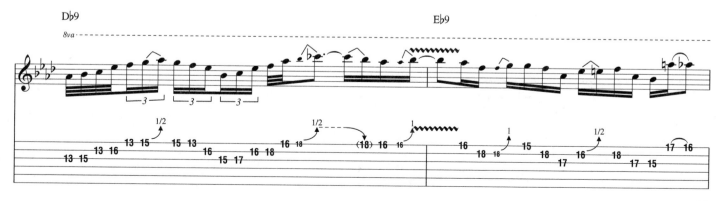

83

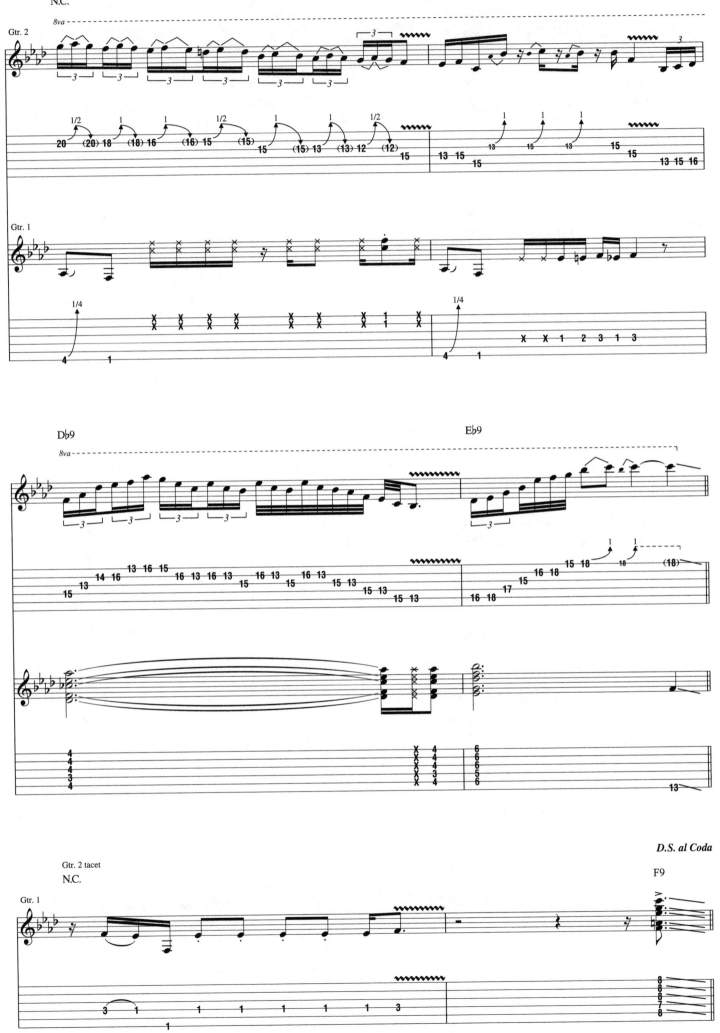

⊕ Coda

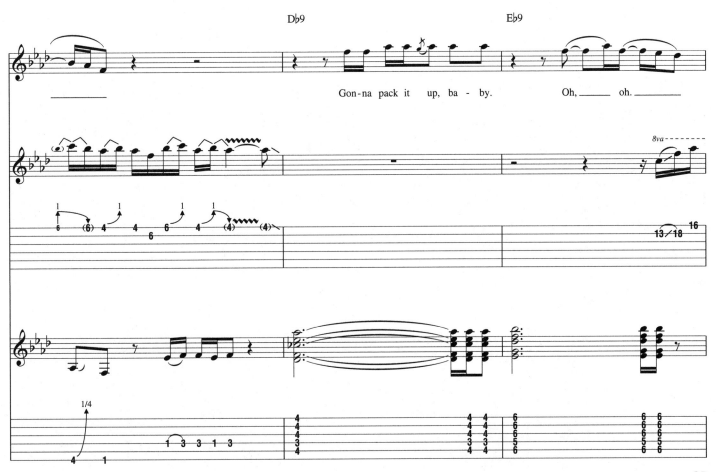

Yeah, I'm gon - na pack it up.

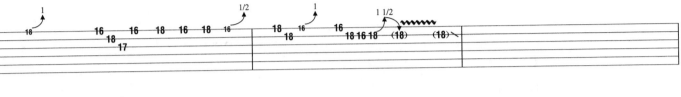

Oh, ——— Lord.

LEFT OVERS

By Albert Collins

*Chord symbols reflect overall harmony.

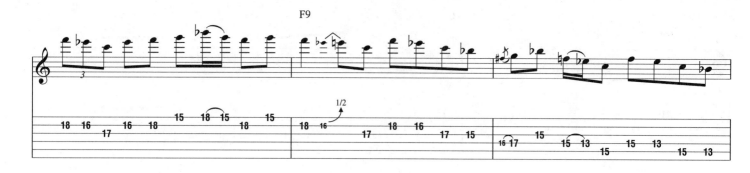

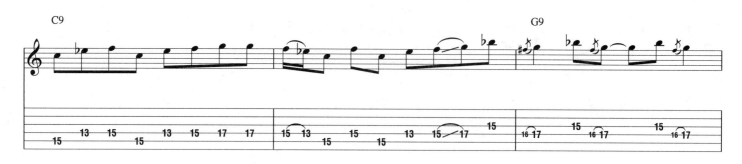

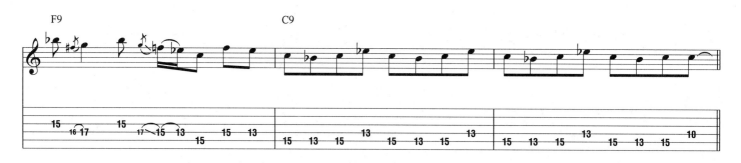

90

Keyboard Solo
Gtr. 1: w/ Rhy. Fig. 1

C7#9

D.C. al Coda
(with repeat)

Coda

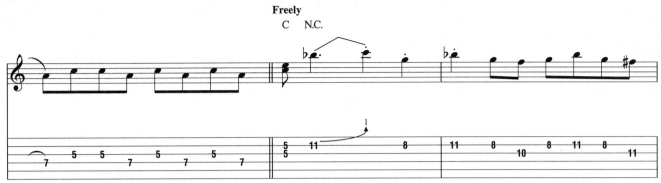

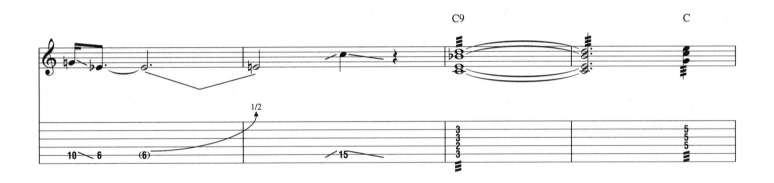

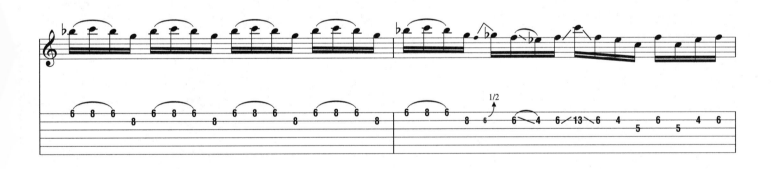

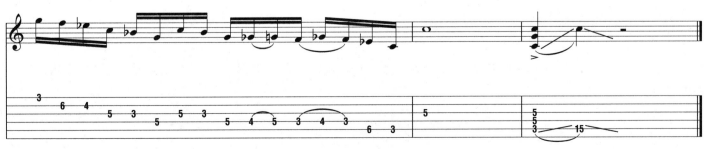

WALKIN' BLUES

Words and Music by
Robert Johnson

Open G tuning:
(low to high) D-G-D-G-B-D

Intro
Moderate Blues/Rock ♩ = 104

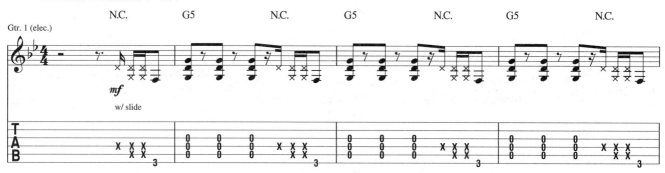

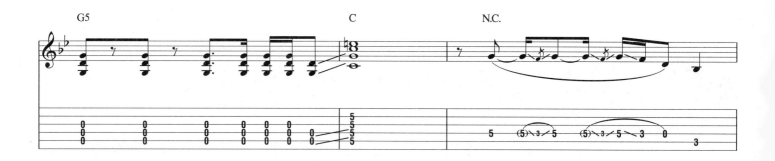

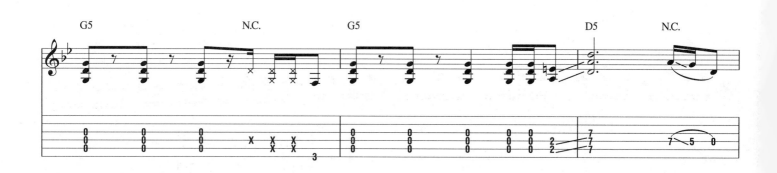

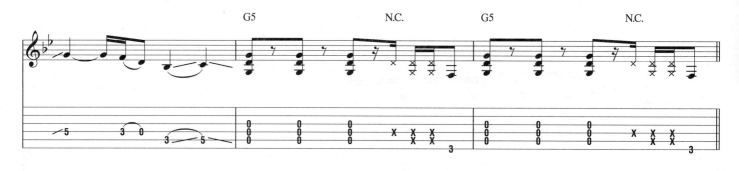

*Chord symbols reflect overall harmony (next 10 meas.).

96

yeah, _____ and I don't mind dy - ing. _

Aw, take it, John.

*Chord symbols reflect overall harmony (next 10 meas.).

Verse

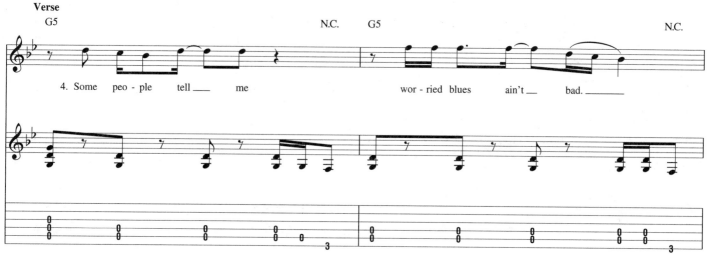

4. Some peo - ple tell ___ me ___ wor - ried blues ain't ___ bad. _____

Worst ___ old feel - ing ___ ev - er had. _____ And ah, ___

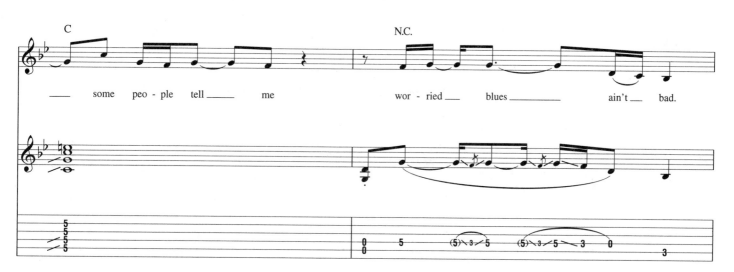

___ some peo - ple tell ___ me ___ wor - ried ___ blues ___ ain't ___ bad.

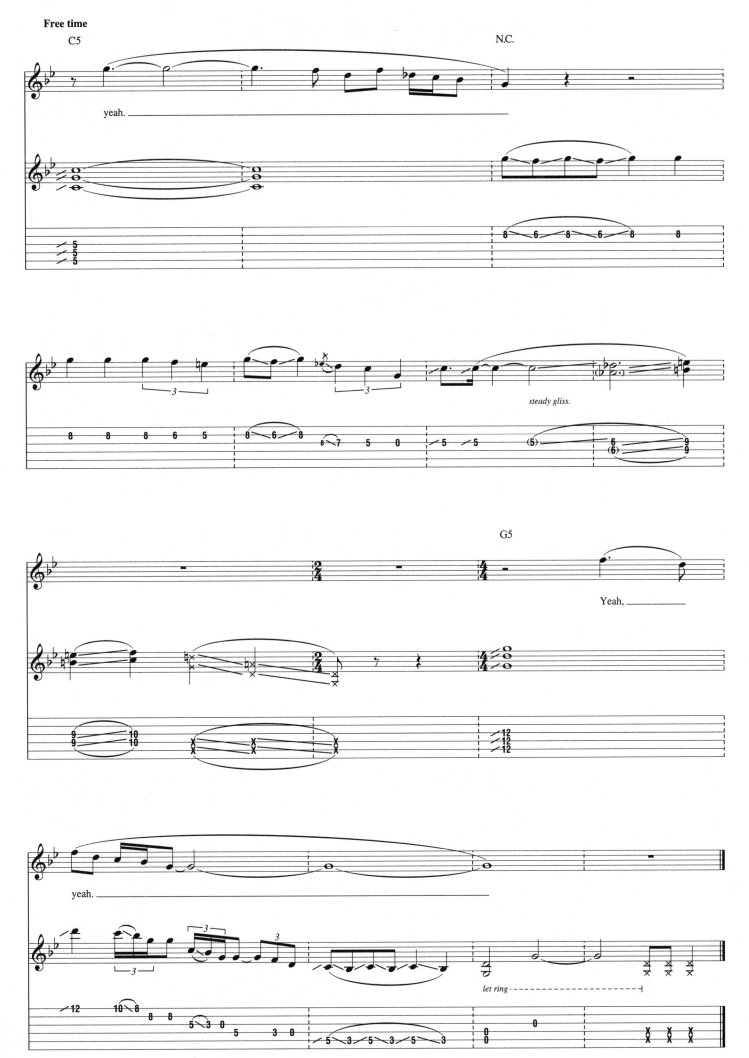

MUMBLING WORD

Words and Music by
Joe Bonamassa and Michael Himelstein

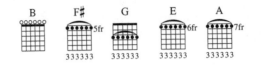

Capo IV
Open E tuning:
(low to high) E-B-E-G#-B-E

Intro
Moderate Blues ♩ = 61

*12-string acoustic steel-string guitar
**All music sounds a major 3rd higher than indicated due to capo. Capoed fret is "0" in tab.

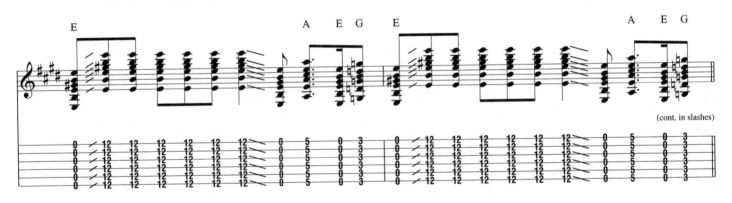

Verse

1. Ba-by, when I   heard those ug-ly things __   that came out of your pret-ty lit-tle mouth, __
2. You   see, it does-n't mat-ter now, _____   what   real-ly good it all ____ would do, __

I   packed up   my beat up suit-case   and took the first train __   south. __
to chap-ter and verse those heart-aches. __   that I been hurt-ing o-ver you. __

Chorus

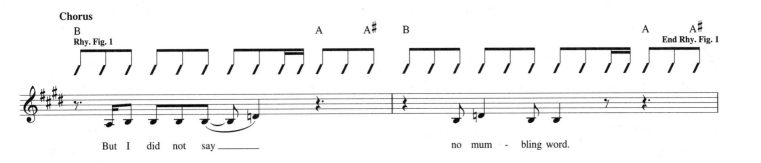

But I did not say _____ no mum - bling word.

Gtr. 1: w/ Rhy. Fig. 1 (2 times)

Not a mum - bling word _____ did I _____ say. _____

But I did not say _____ no mum - bling word.

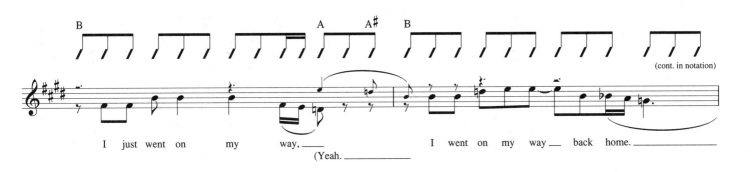

(cont. in notation)

I just went on my way, _____ I went on my way __ back home. _____
(Yeah. _____

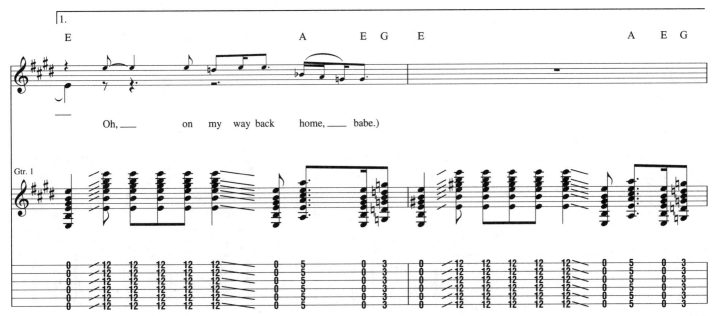

Oh, __ on my way back home, ___ babe.)

Gtr. 1

Yeah.

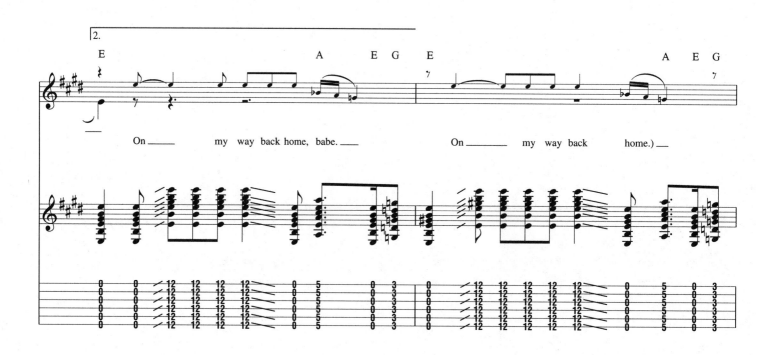

On _____ my way back home, babe. _____ On _____ my way back home.) _____

Yeah.

(cont. in slashes)

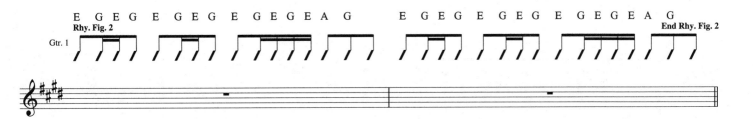

Bridge

Now, __ I was-n't run-nin', lit-tle la - dy. __ I set the rec - ord nice and __ straight.

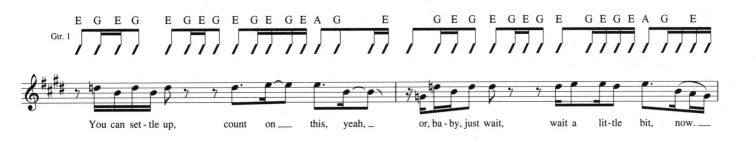

You can set - tle up, count on __ this, yeah, __ or, ba - by, just wait, wait a lit-tle bit, now. __

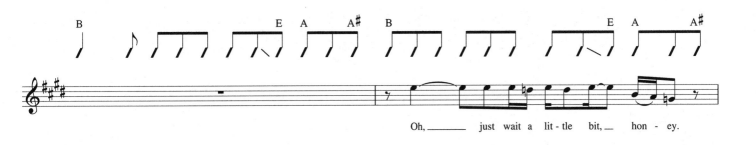

Oh, _____ just wait a lit - tle bit, __ hon - ey.

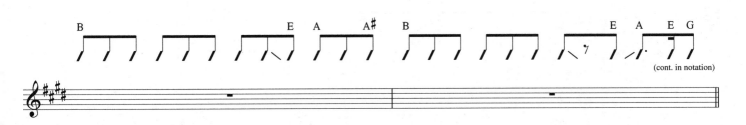

(cont. in notation)

Outro

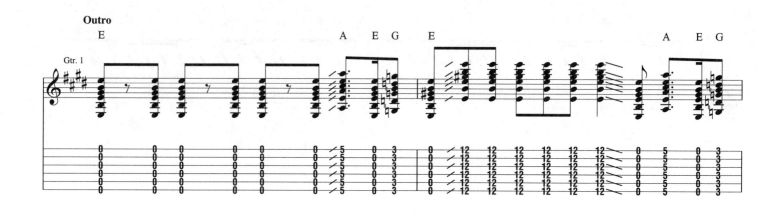

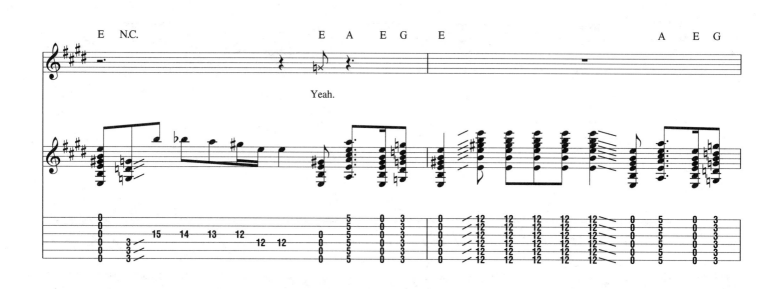

Yeah.

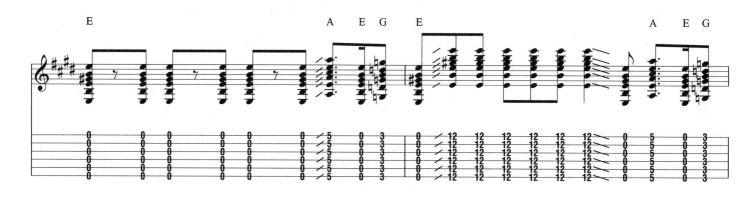

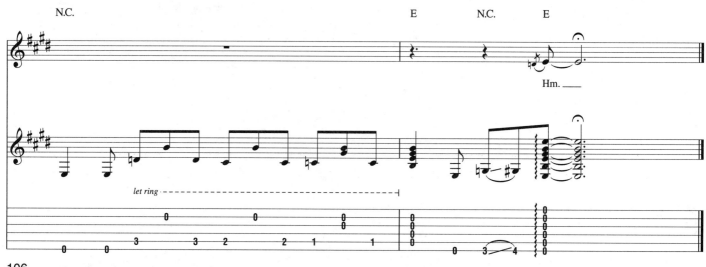

Hm. ____

PAIN AND SORROW

Words and Music by
Joe Bonamassa, Richard Feldman
and Eric Pressly

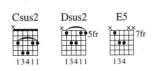

Tune down 1 step:
(low to high) D-G-C-F-A-D

Intro
Free time (slowly)

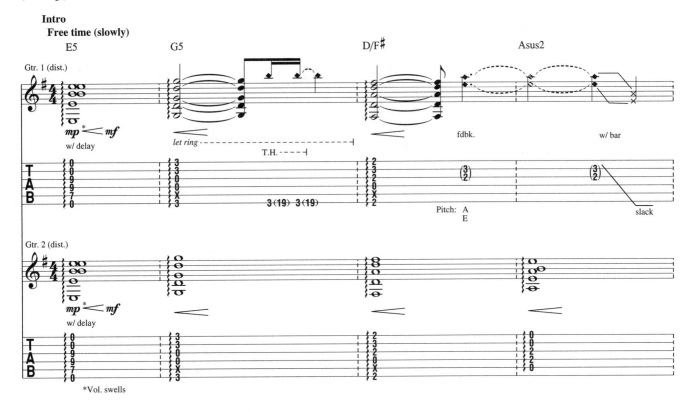

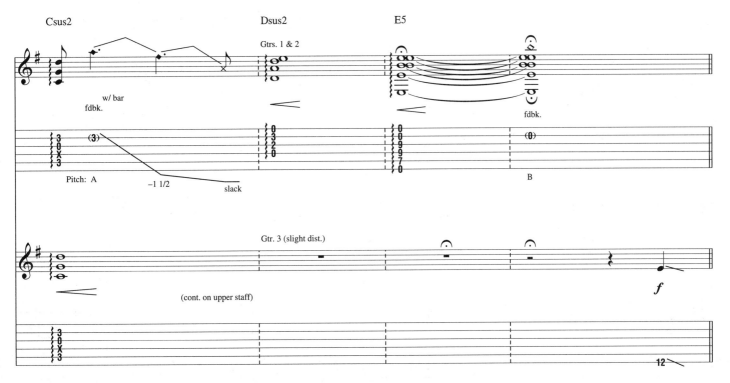

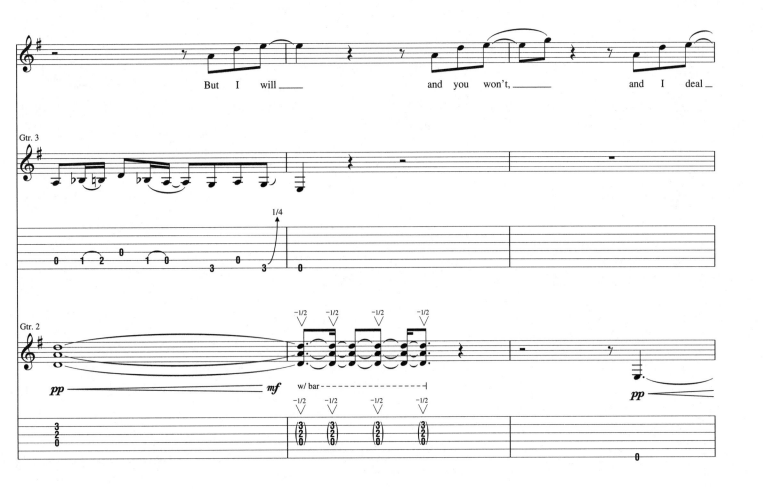

But I will ____ and you won't, _____ and I deal __

Gtr. 3

Gtr. 2

pp ____ mf w/ bar - - - - - - - - - - - - - - - pp

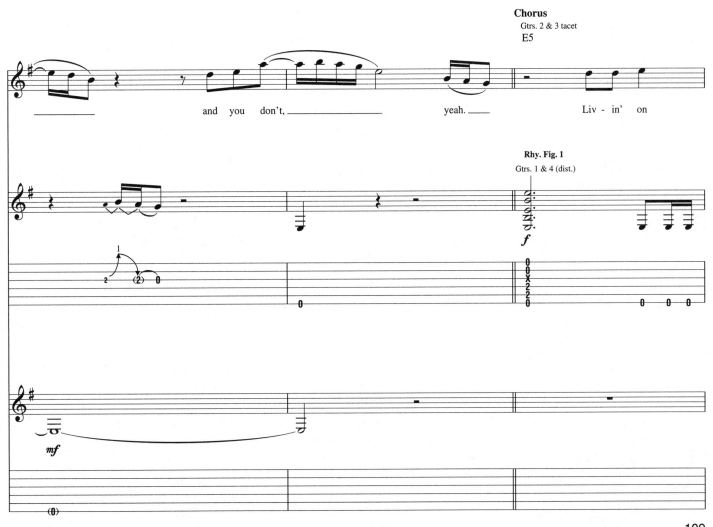

Chorus
Gtrs. 2 & 3 tacet
E5

____ and you don't, _____ yeah. ____ Liv - in' on

Rhy. Fig. 1
Gtrs. 1 & 4 (dist.)

f

mf

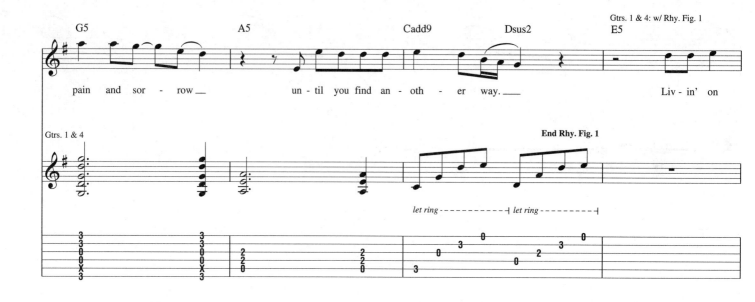

pain and sor - row __ un - til you find an - oth - er way. __ Liv - in' on

pain and sor - row __ un - til I find an - oth - er way. __

Verse

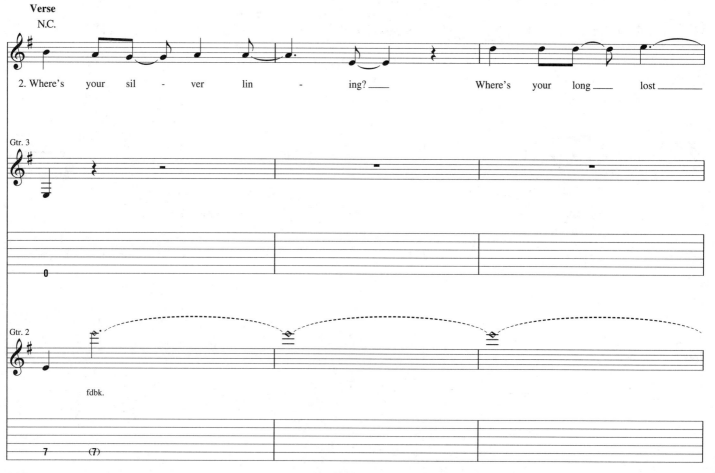

2. Where's your sil - ver lin - ing? __ Where's your long __ lost __

_____ friend? _____   The emp - ti - ness _____ is shin - ing _____ from

some - where deep _____ with - in.   But I will _____ and you won't, _

w/ hybrid picking

pp ——————— mf

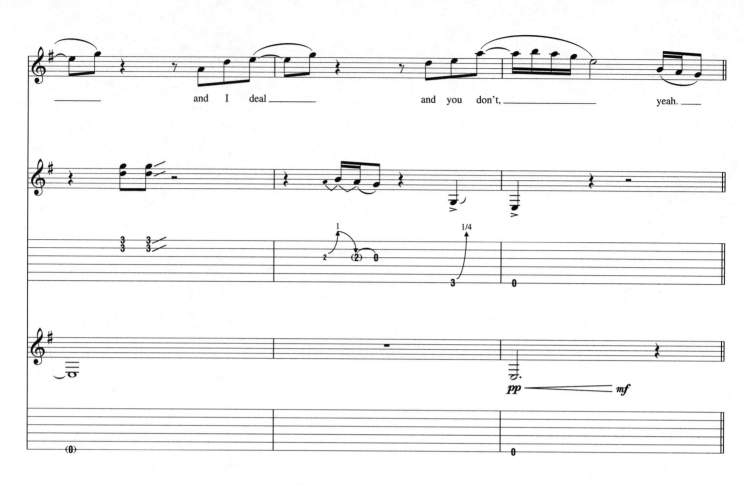

Chorus

Gtrs. 2 & 3 tacet
Gtrs. 1 & 4: w/ Rhy. Fig. 1 (4 times)

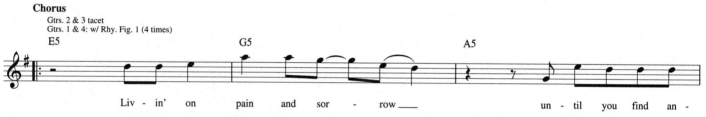

E5   G5   A5

Liv - in' on pain and sor - row ____ un - til you find an -

Cadd9   Dsus2   E5   G5

oth - er way. ____ Liv - in' on pain and sor - row ____

Gtr. 3: w/ Riff A (4 times)

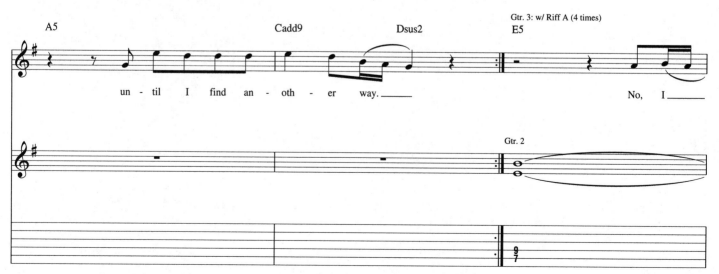

A5   Cadd9   Dsus2   E5

un - til I find an - oth - er way. ____ No, I ____

Gtr. 2

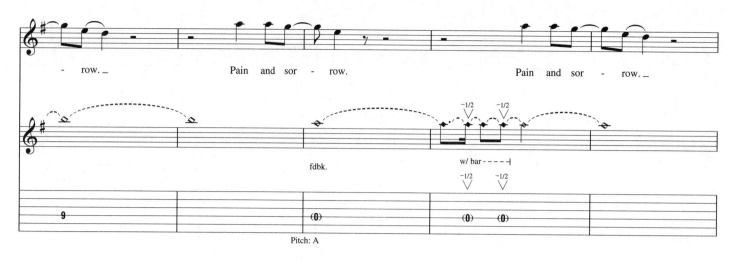

- row. ___   Pain and sor - row.   Pain and sor - row. ___

fdbk.

Pitch: A

End double-time feel

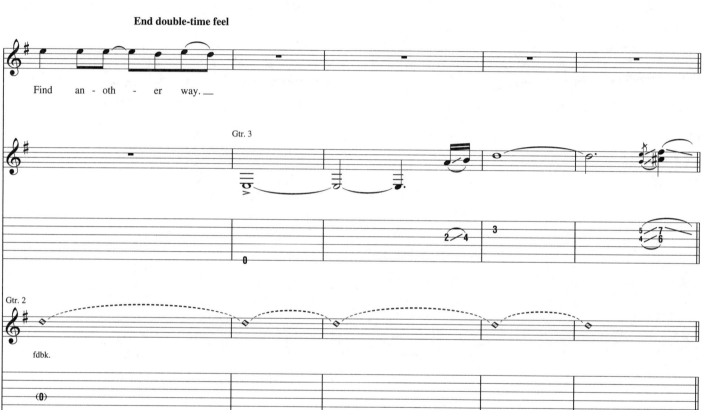

Find an - oth - er way. ___

Gtr. 3

Gtr. 2

fdbk.

Guitar Solo

N.C.(E5)

P.M.

Rhy. Fig. 2

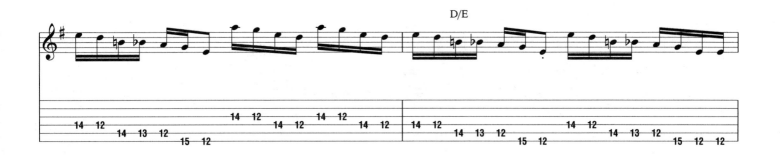

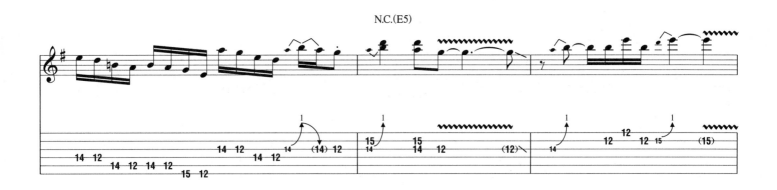

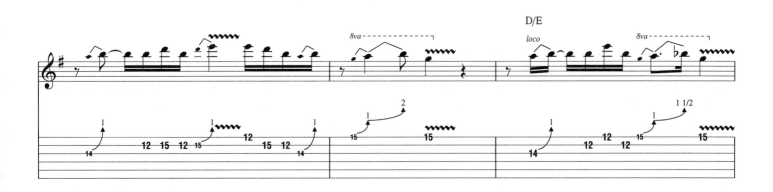

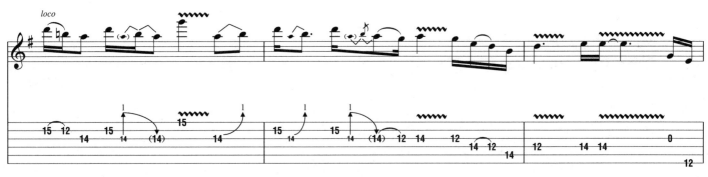

N.C.(E5)

D/E

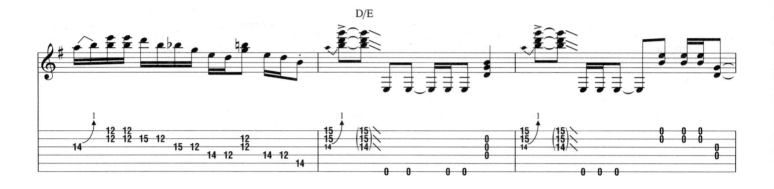

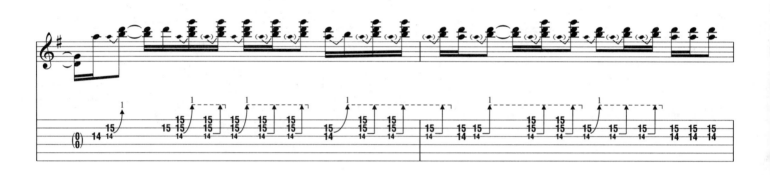

Gtr. 2: w/ Rhy. Fig. 2 (1st 4 meas.)
N.C.(E5)

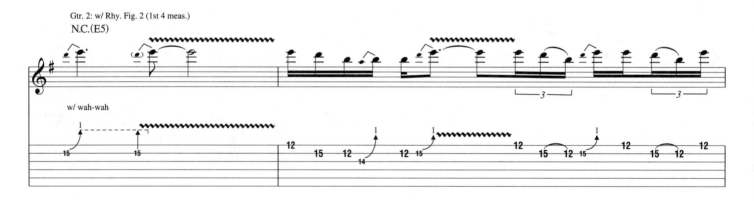

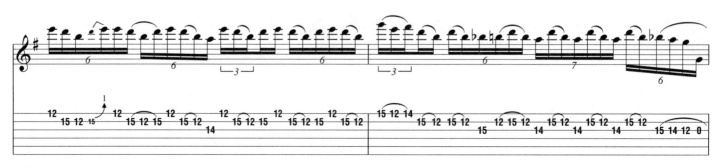

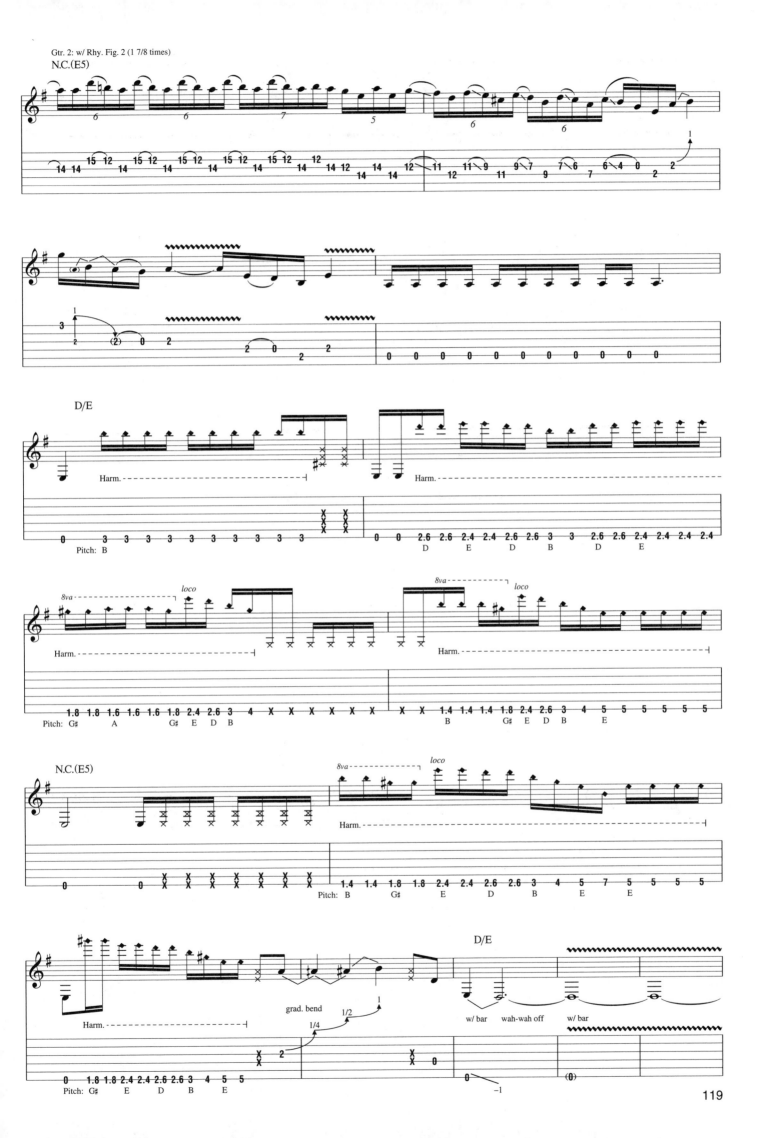

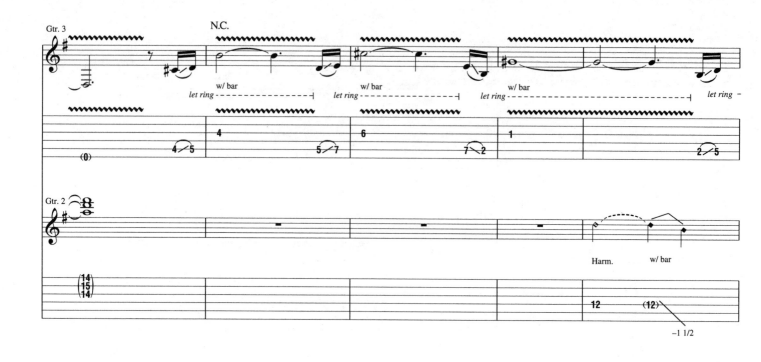

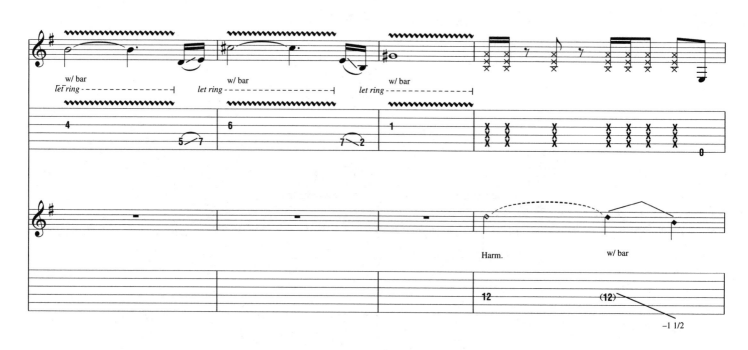

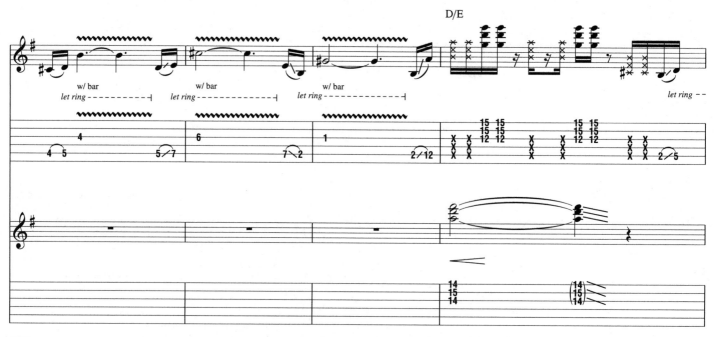

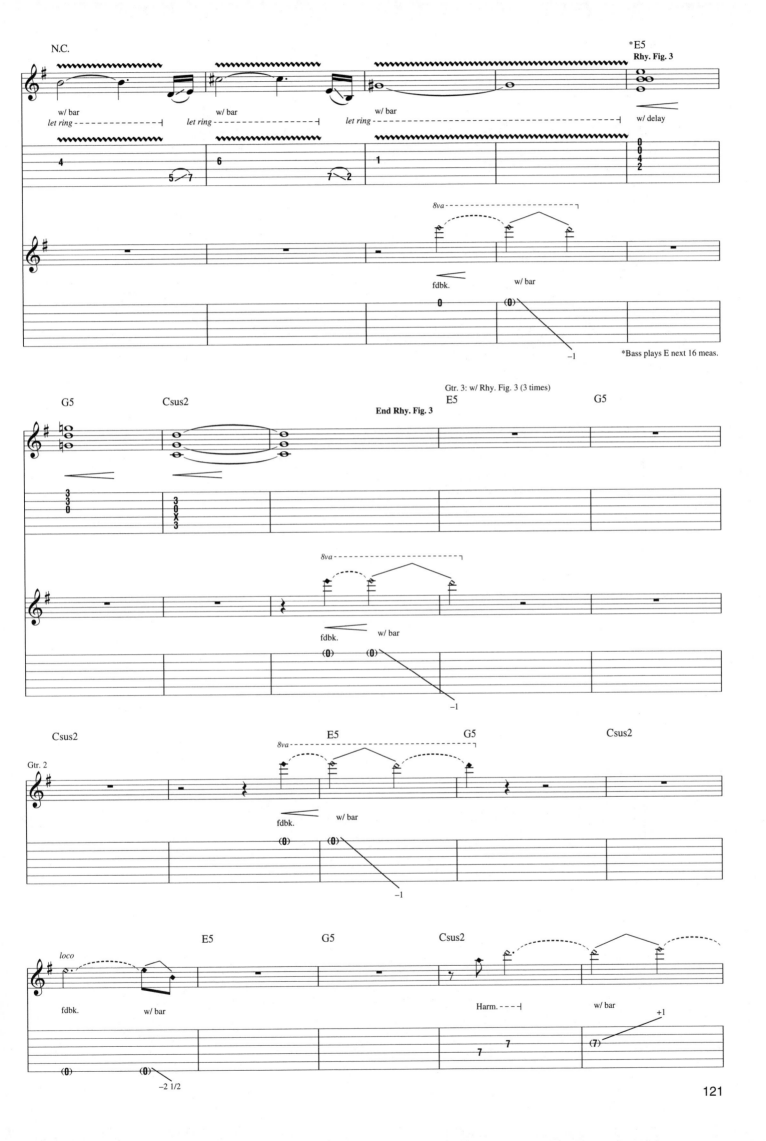

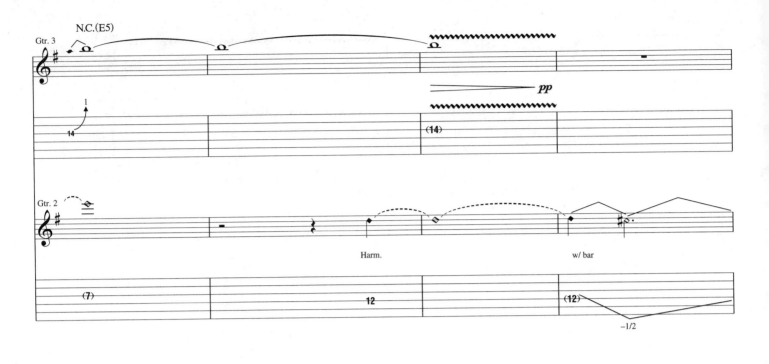

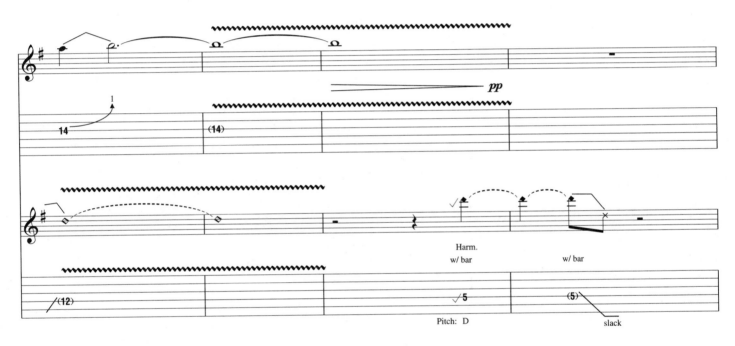

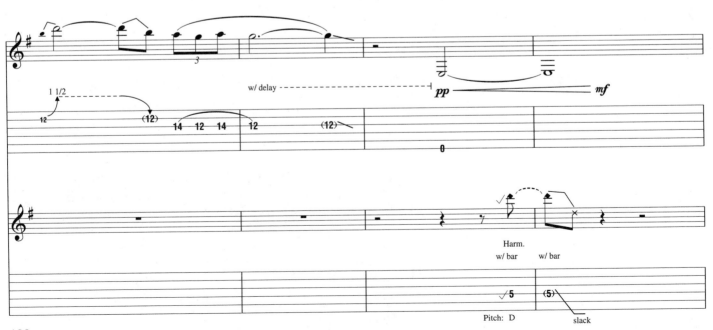

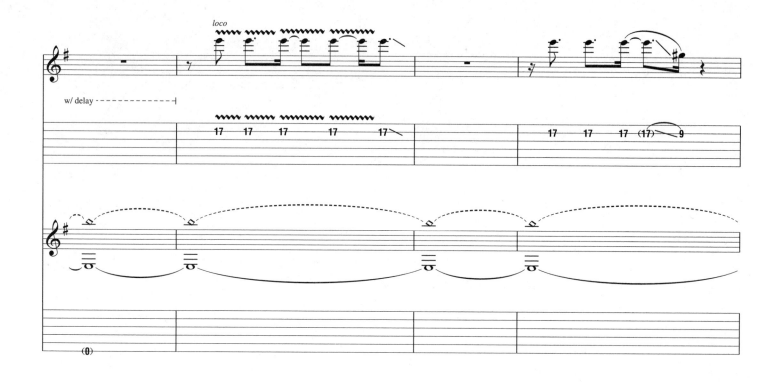

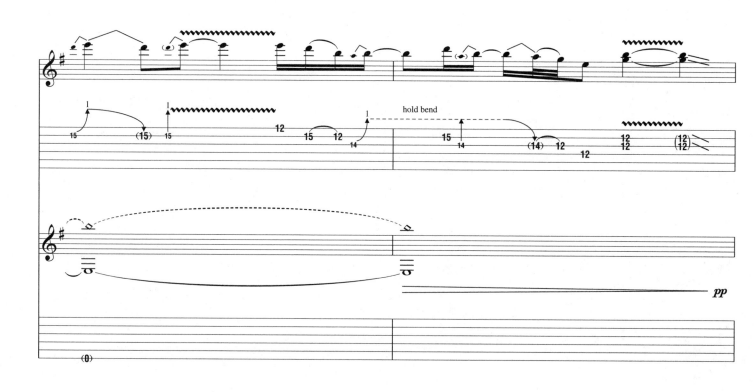

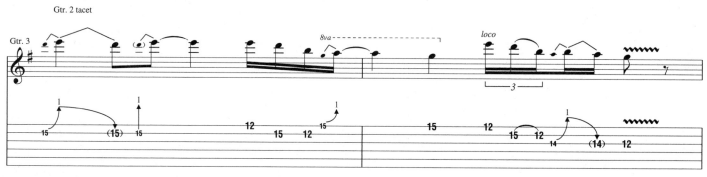

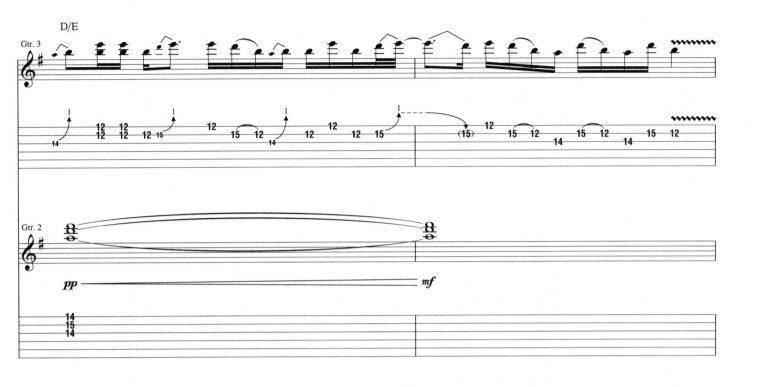

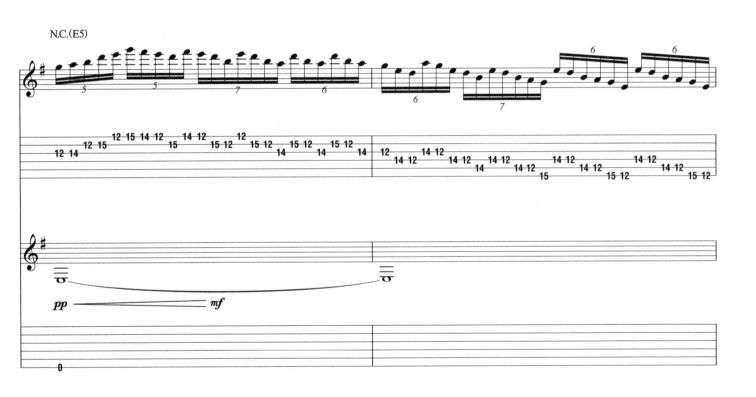

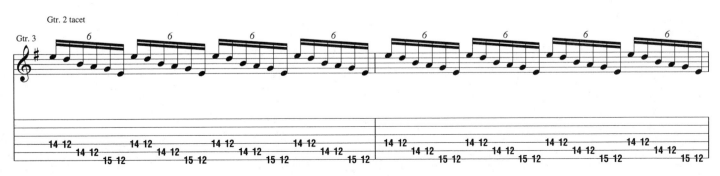

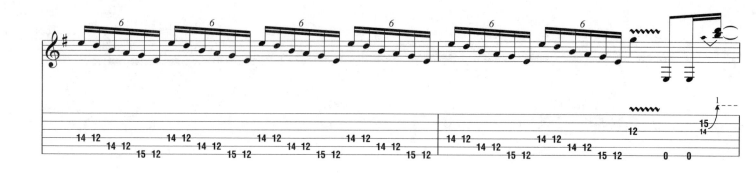

D/E

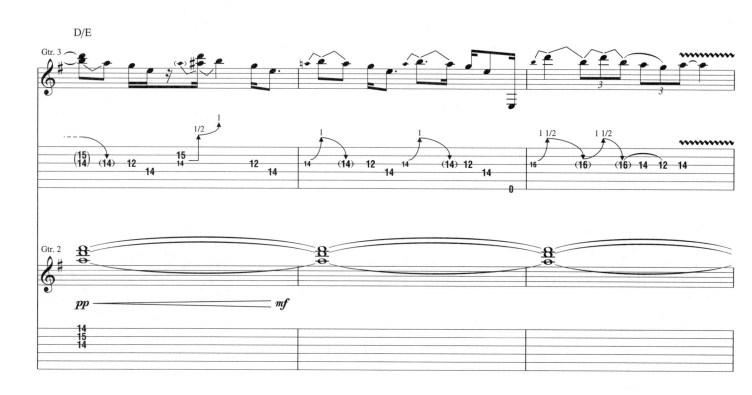

N.C.(E5)

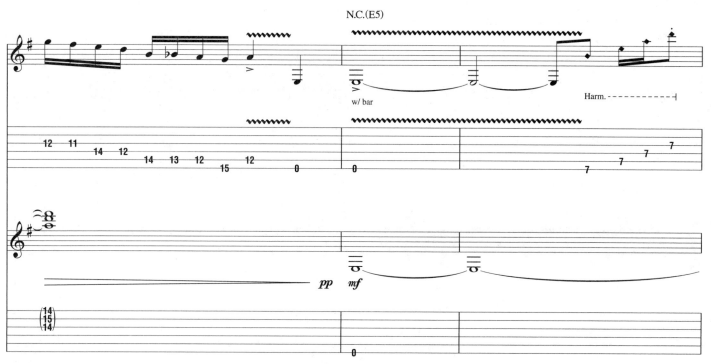

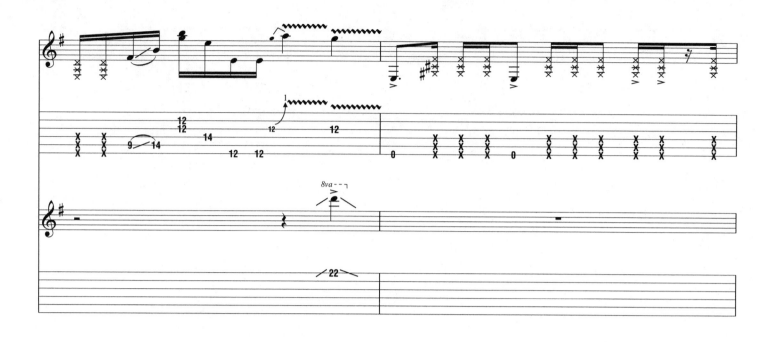

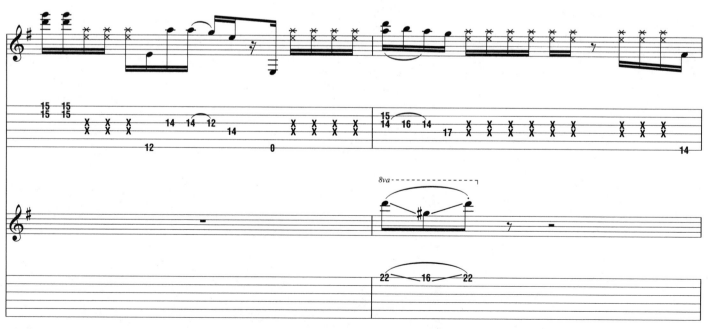

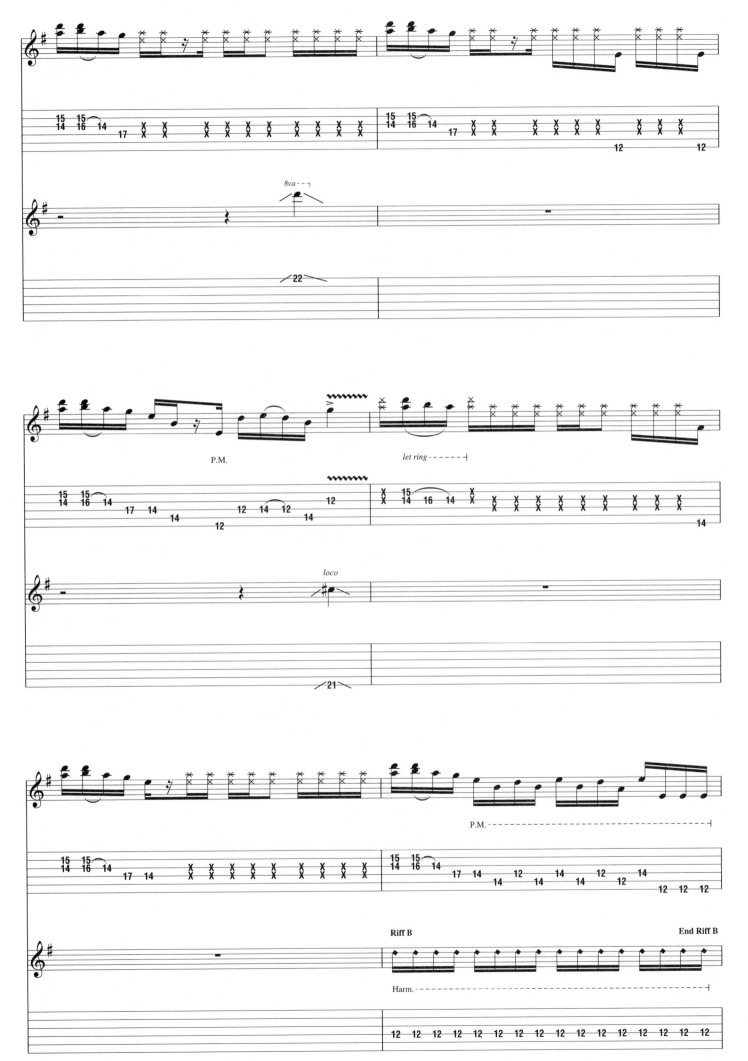

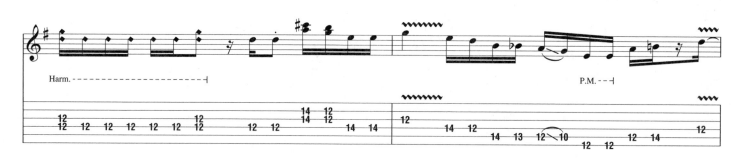

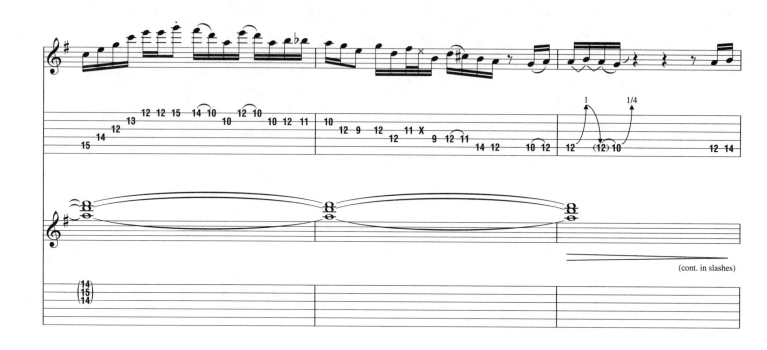

Csus2   Dsus2   E5
Rhy. Fig. 3

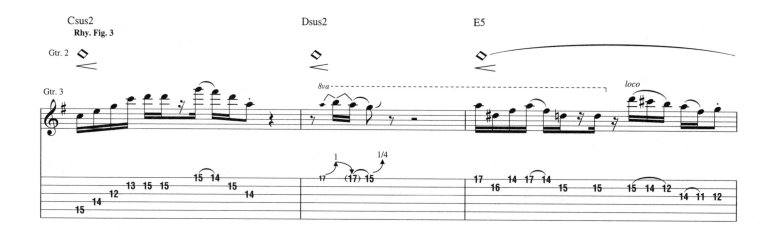

Gtr. 2: w/ Rhy. Fig. 3 (5 1/2 times)
Csus2
End Rhy. Fig. 3

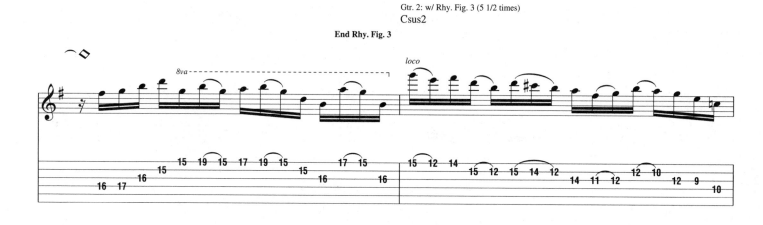

Dsus2   E5

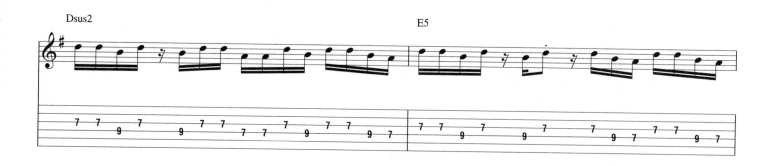

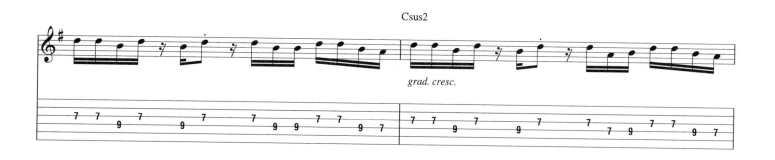

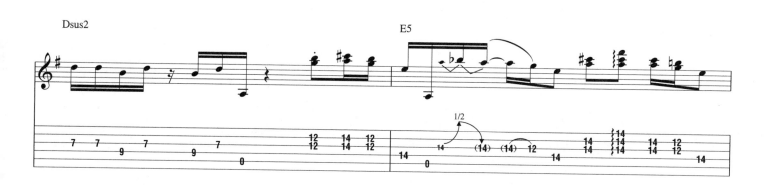

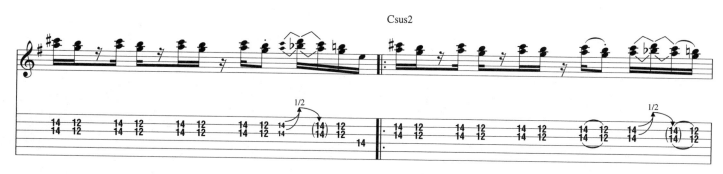

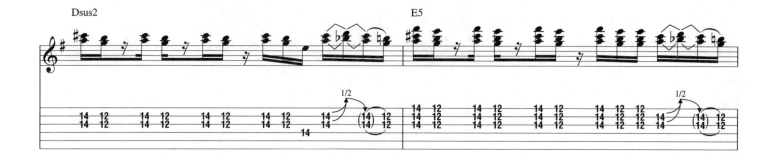

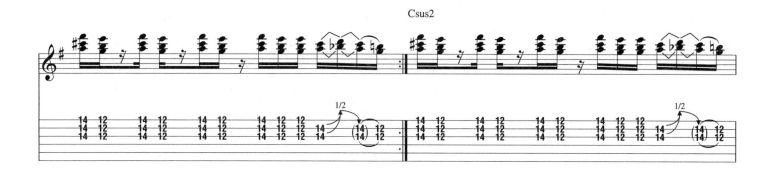

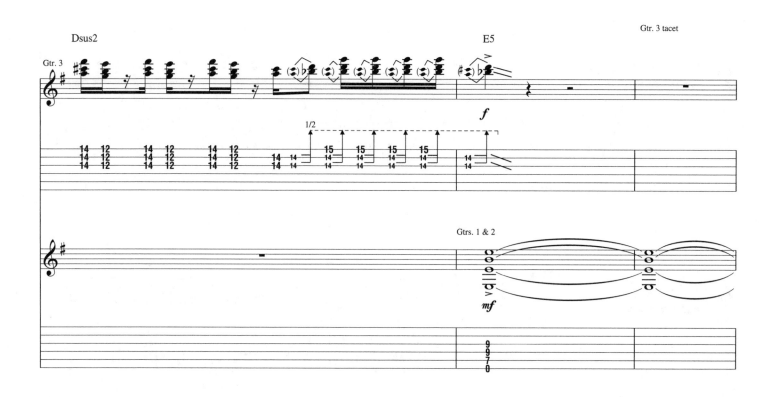

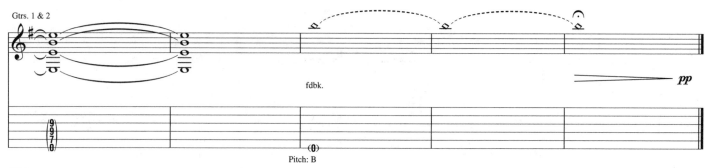

Guitar Notation Legend

Guitar music can be notated three different ways: on a *musical staff*, in *tablature*, and in *rhythm slashes*.

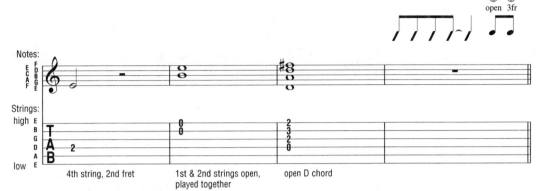

RHYTHM SLASHES are written above the staff. Strum chords in the rhythm indicated. Use the chord diagrams found at the top of the first page of the transcription for the appropriate chord voicings. Round noteheads indicate single notes.

THE MUSICAL STAFF shows pitches and rhythms and is divided by bar lines into measures. Pitches are named after the first seven letters of the alphabet.

TABLATURE graphically represents the guitar fingerboard. Each horizontal line represents a string, and each number represents a fret.

HALF-STEP BEND: Strike the note and bend up 1/2 step.

WHOLE-STEP BEND: Strike the note and bend up one step.

GRACE NOTE BEND: Strike the note and immediately bend up as indicated.

SLIGHT (MICROTONE) BEND: Strike the note and bend up 1/4 step.

BEND AND RELEASE: Strike the note and bend up as indicated, then release back to the original note. Only the first note is struck.

PRE-BEND: Bend the note as indicated, then strike it.

VIBRATO: The string is vibrated by rapidly bending and releasing the note with the fretting hand.

WIDE VIBRATO: The pitch is varied to a greater degree by vibrating with the fretting hand.

HAMMER-ON: Strike the first (lower) note with one finger, then sound the higher note (on the same string) with another finger by fretting it without picking.

PULL-OFF: Place both fingers on the notes to be sounded. Strike the first note and without picking, pull the finger off to sound the second (lower) note.

LEGATO SLIDE: Strike the first note and then slide the same fret-hand finger up or down to the second note. The second note is not struck.

SHIFT SLIDE: Same as legato slide, except the second note is struck.

TRILL: Very rapidly alternate between the notes indicated by continuously hammering on and pulling off.

TAPPING: Hammer ("tap") the fret indicated with the pick-hand index or middle finger and pull off to the note fretted by the fret hand.

NATURAL HARMONIC: Strike the note while the fret-hand lightly touches the string directly over the fret indicated.

PINCH HARMONIC: The note is fretted normally and a harmonic is produced by adding the edge of the thumb or the tip of the index finger of the pick hand to the normal pick attack.

PICK SCRAPE: The edge of the pick is rubbed down (or up) the string, producing a scratchy sound.

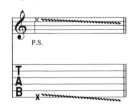

MUFFLED STRINGS: A percussive sound is produced by laying the fret hand across the string(s) without depressing, and striking them with the pick hand.

PALM MUTING: The note is partially muted by the pick hand lightly touching the string(s) just before the bridge.

RAKE: Drag the pick across the strings indicated with a single motion.

TREMOLO PICKING: The note is picked as rapidly and continuously as possible.

VIBRATO BAR DIVE AND RETURN: The pitch of the note or chord is dropped a specified number of steps (in rhythm), then returned to the original pitch.

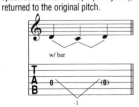

VIBRATO BAR SCOOP: Depress the bar just before striking the note, then quickly release the bar.

VIBRATO BAR DIP: Strike the note and then immediately drop a specified number of steps, then release back to the original pitch.

135

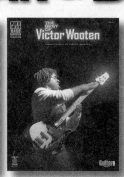